366 Brief Prayers for Your Church Community

by
James J. Stewart

© 2020 James J. Stewart
ISBN: 978-1-7326609-9-1

My heart-felt thanks to Beth,
who suggested compiling this book of
prayers based upon my entries for
Facebook and other social media.

**366 Brief Prayers for your Church Community,
enough for one prayer each day**

5

Heavenly Father, we believe by faith, You are gloriously at work among us, using us for Your awesome glory. For this & much more we are thankful. We are amazed You love us despite ourselves because Jesus died for our sins. Help us stay focused upon You in the midst of the messes we make. We surrender our often-chaotic lives to You in the name of Your Son, Jesus. Amen.

2

Merciful God, sometimes we feel so immersed in this sin-filled world that we hunger for Your presence and truly long to see You glorified. Thank You for being forgiving and patient. Help us cope with attacks on Christianity and Your church in the media and elsewhere. Teach us how to serve You better on Your terms, Your way, we pray in Jesus' name. Amen.

3

Gracious God, all of Your creation is beautiful, from the sounds of singing birds to lakes and meadows dressed in fog. We don't stop to appreciate Your glory enough. Thank You for giving us the ability to smell our favorite foods and the privilege of praying through the night. Help us to respond to the needs around us more lovingly and graciously. We surrender our own needs to You through Jesus, Amen.

4

Ever-present God, we have our limits and don't know all that You do. Thank You for being so patient and merciful to us. Please keep our eyes open to where You're leading us. We ask that You be our shield and fortress for all of us as a community of faith. Thank You for hearing our prayers for healing, mercy, and grace. We praise and love You in Jesus' name. Amen.

6

Eternal God, we praise and worship You because we're in awe of You and of all of Your creation. We don't deserve Your loving mercy. Thank You for delivering another tomorrow, another chance. Please comfort those in pain and heal them, and please redeem us all that we may effectively serve You. We humbly offer this prayer in Jesus' name. Amen.

6

All-knowing God, Your glorious work among us is amazing, as You bind us together with Your eternal love. During the pandemic, we have not been focused enough on You and helping others. We're thankful that You never give up upon Your children. Please help us to prepare for being physically united again, to worship You with fellowship. We surrender the challenges we are facing to You, and we pray this in the power of Jesus' name, Amen.

7

Heavenly Father, we know we need Your forgiveness and grace. Forgive us when we are afraid instead of trusting You. Thank You for bringing us this far, delivering us from so much evil in our world. Help us stay focused upon You as we begin to open up our lives again and share with one another in fellowship. We gladly surrender it all to You in Jesus' name. Amen.

8

Loving God, Your patience and mercy are as amazing as Your grace. We are unworthy of Your reckless love. Thank You for another chance to walk with Jesus today. Teach us to live as well as pray in Jesus' name. Help our community of faith to be more like Our Savior and Lord. We surrender all that we are and have to You in the power of Jesus' name. Amen.

Gracious God, we weren't ready for Covid-19, and we still have some fear of what is to come. Thank You for sustaining us and being our shield and fortress. Please guide and empower us to be Your church in the weeks and months ahead. We surrender our fears to You, for You are greater than our fears as You continue to love us. In the power of Jesus' name we pray. Amen.

10

Heavenly Father, as we prepare to reopen our doors, we surrender our concerns for the future of our spiritual community to You. We ask that You multiply our efforts to serve You and to worship You. Thank You for those who have gone before us to create and build our church. We confess we could do more than we are doing. We love You and praise You in the name of Jesus, who is our Savior, best friend, and constant companion. Amen.

11

Eternal and humbling God, we love and adore You. Our faith is often weak, but You are our strength. We're so grateful that You have never given up on us. We ask for Your healing and redemption for those we know to be sick or in pain. We surrender them and ourselves to Your power and love and ask that you heal us and redeem us in Jesus' name. Amen.

12

Awesome God, You are our amazing shield and fortress, who sets and defends our boundaries. We offer You our allegiance, gracious God. With you on our side, we have no excuse to be scared amidst the chaos around us. Thank You for being our good shepherd. We lift up to You our family and friends who have gone astray, and we surrender them in our prayers to Your perfect timing in Jesus' name. Amen.

8

Loving heavenly Father, we need Your forgiveness and grace. We love communing with You, our glorious God, in prayer and worship. Thank You for being so patient and kind towards us. Help us to see the path You have prepared for each of us clearly. We surrender all that we are and have to You in the name of Your only-begotten son, Jesus. Amen.

14

Lord, we see the wondrous beauty of Your creation all around us. We don't express our praise and appreciation enough. We're careful what we pray for because You are so graciously willing to answer. Thank You for the ability to perceive so much of You around us. Please multiply our efforts to do Your will and be Your church. We surrender to You the challenges we face in Jesus' name. Amen.

15

Jesus, we surrender our family and friends to You. Some of them can be difficult to love, so help us to love all of them as You teach us to do. Thank You for showing us how to serve You on Your terms and in Your way. We're sorry when we are inconsistent in our praise and love for You. To You belongs all the praise and glory through Jesus. Amen.

16

Heavenly Father, we cannot praise You enough or even begin to love You as much as You love us. Your eternal forgiving love is but one aspect of Your amazing grace. We often stumble and fail to be faithful. Thank You for filling our real needs, even while we greedily want more. Please increase our faith and our trust in You. We surrender to You, just as we are, in Jesus' name. Amen.

9

Gracious God, we want You to be in control, guiding us. Forgive us when we go our own way. We serve You Your way, Lord God, because You called us. Please help us make, mature, and multiply more faithful disciples of Jesus. Thank You for giving us more chances to do Your will. We want to do better. Your unrelenting love and grace are amazing. In Jesus' name we pray, Amen.

18

Holy Father in heaven, we honor and adore You with our worship. We know Your Son shed his blood to wash away our sins, but we need Your forgiveness every day. Thank You for multiplying our efforts to serve You. We ask for healing for those we know who need an extra measure of Your grace. We surrender their pain and suffering to Your care in Jesus' name. Amen.

19

Christ our King, You rule our community of faith with mercy and grace. Please help us grow into becoming more like You as we follow You. Thank You for being our rock, our fortress, and our deliverer. We are surrounded with temptations and depend upon You to save us. We're devoted to You and adore You, Lord Jesus, for it is in Your name we pray. Amen.

20

Gracious God, we are in awe of You, for You are glorious. We cling to Your mercy and grace, knowing that You sent Jesus to save us. Thank You for the saints before us that made our current community of faith possible. Please strengthen our efforts to move forward with Your nurture and guidance. You hold our future through Jesus, our Savior. Amen.

10

Gracious and powerful God, we joyfully take in the beauty of all of Your creation. It reminds us both of Your perfection, and of our failures that You redeem through Jesus' blood. Thank You for not giving up on us and giving us more chances. Help us strain out the truth from the waterfall of words from our media. We stand on Your promises, depending on You, in Jesus' name. Amen.

22

Almighty God, we love You. We do things we didn't intend to do, and we don't do the things we should. Thank You for being so patient with us. Your loving kindness and severity are in perfect balance. As we look forward to next Sunday's community worship, please bind us together with Your eternal love. All that we are and have are in Your care, through Jesus our Lord, we pray. Amen.

23

Our Father, we are Yours, and we want to serve You Your way. You are gloriously our Savior, best friend, and always-present God. We ask for the vision to perceive Your will and increased faith to trust you with everything. Thank You for helping us grow in our faith. We still are making mistakes and need Your forgiveness. All praise and glory belong to You, through Jesus, our Master. Amen.

24

Amazing and awesome God, our every thought is known to You. Please forgive us when our thoughts turn to evil and away from our gracious God. Thank You for hearing our prayers and responding out of Your kindness and mercy. We pray for our family and friends who haven't accepted Jesus as their Savior, that they may come to know Him. We surrender them into Your hands in the name of Jesus, our Savior and Lord. Amen.

11

Merciful God, we grieve with You over those who respond to violent injustice with rage and more injustice. If we have turned a blind eye to such sin, please forgive us. You alone are all that is good and right. Thank You for protecting Your innocent children we know. Be our shield and fortress and guide us to respond faithfully to Your leading we ask in Jesus' name. Amen.

26

Father, we praise You seven days, not just Sundays. We need Your mercy and grace every day. Thank You for hearing our prayers, even when we don't quickly see the answers. Sometimes our troubles almost seem to overwhelm us. Please let each of us walk each day with Jesus as our constant companion. We offer this prayer in Jesus' name. Amen.

27

Glorious God, please forgive us when we're tempted with extreme responses to evil which could be as bad as the evil we witness. Thank You for being our shield and fortress that shelter us from the storms of life. Grant us, we pray, the wisdom to respond effectively to the many needs around us. Use us for Your glory, we ask in Jesus' name. Amen.

28

Lovingly patient God, we're thrilled with the new life that constantly grows around us. We're sorry we often don't notice the evidence of Your work in our midst. Thank You for the everyday blessings we too easily take for granted. Please show us how to live out Your plans and purposes for our lives in better ways. We offer ourselves to You in Jesus' name. Amen.

29

Deliver us, Lord God, for the world around us seems out of control. We know You are in command, and we thank You for hearing our prayers. Every day we read of people responding to evil with their own evil. We confess we're tempted to respond with unrighteous anger. We kneel before You and worship, for You are the creator and redeemer of all. In the name of our Lord Jesus, we pray. Amen.

30

Beloved Lord, our amazing God, we're so often weak, but You are always strong. When our faith falters, You pick us up. Thank You for being so patient with us. Please teach us to worry less and trust You more, both as individuals and as a community. We look to our Jesus that we follow. We're trying to be like Him, and we pray this in His name. Amen.

31

Heavenly Father, our praise goes beyond Sunday mornings and into the entire week. Our shortcomings are manifested every day, so we are thankful we're forgiven through Jesus' blood shed on the cross. It seems we've been walking in the valley of the shadow, so please lead us with Your everlasting light. We lay our burdens before You in Jesus' name. Amen.

32

We yield to Your divine authority, O God. Please show us Your way into our future. We're grateful that You have delivered us from so much evil and thankful we are so abundantly blessed. We certainly don't deserve all that You provide us out of Your abundant love. Help us to seek those who need Jesus and disciple them. We praise You and glorify You in the name of Your Son Jesus. Amen.

13

Awesome and amazing Father in heaven, we don't have Your patience, and sometimes we just don't want to forgive politicians and others who keep us from moving forward. Thank You for teaching us Your better ways. Please guide us past the maze of lies and other evils that assault our lives. You are our fortress, our shield, and our shelter. We give over control into Your almighty hands in Jesus' name. Amen.

34

All praise and glory are Yours, Father, because if You had not sent Jesus to die for us, we would be so utterly lost in this temptation-filled world. We are so grateful that You deliver us from evil and guide us through our world's chaos. Increase our faith, Father, and strengthen us to do Your will, fulfilling the plans and purpose You have for us. We surrender to You, just as we are, in Jesus' name. Amen.

35

Gracious and merciful Lord, we praise Your compassion towards us, how You are slow to be angry with us and love us anyway as we are, not counting our sins against us. Thank You for being ready to forgive us once more whenever we ask. Grant us faith that is warm, strong, peaceful, and compassionate, as we offer ourselves to You once again in Jesus' name. Amen.

36

Beautiful Creator and Savior, so often we sin against You, not just in what we do, but even in what we think and say. So often we fail to love You and each other unconditionally. Please mercifully forgive us through Jesus, our Savior. Help us to find real joy in walking with Jesus, for we want to be completely His and faithfully witness as You glorify Yourself in us through Jesus. Amen.

14

Master, when we pause to look beyond ourselves, we see the beauty of Your creation all around us. Take away the ugliness in our sinful selves and recreate within us a measure of Your beauty. Thank You for creating this spiritual community where we are both encouraged and held accountable. Help us to make, mature, and multiply more faithful followers of our Lord Jesus, in His name. Amen.

38

All blessings flow from You, O God, so we join countless others in Heaven and on Earth in praising You. We have no excuses for our sins, yet You still mercifully and graciously forgive us. Thank You. Please set us free from our spiritual bondage to the things we love instead of loving You. We surrender our hurts, habits, and hang-ups to You in Jesus' name. Amen.

39

Heavenly Father, we find joy in seeing You glorify Yourself in couples that serve You together. We're also thrilled when You glorify Yourself in single adults focused upon serving and glorifying You. Thank You for providing unique plans and purposes for each of us. We too often lose track of them. Help us to keep growing in You, for we give You all that we are in Jesus' name. Amen.

40

Gloriously awesome God, we love You. Sometimes we act as though we don't know You and know Your ways. Please forgive us. Thank You for abundantly supplying our needs. It is a privilege to live as well as we do. Please provide healing and redemption to those we know need You. We surrender all that we take for granted in Jesus' name. Amen.

Thank You, Heavenly Father, for healing beyond hurt, for Your love beyond measure, for life beyond life, and for the mysteries beyond comprehending that You provide for us. Our love for You seems puny by comparison. We don't deserve Your forgiveness and grace. We adore You. Teach us to work together more effectively as a community of faith. We offer our prayers and ourselves in Jesus' name. Amen.

42

Wondrous Father in heaven, we praise You for common things, like a night full of stars and gentle wind in the trees. We complain too much about things we've given ourselves to do. Thank You for opportunities to laugh and share food and fellowship. Please help us to love the people we don't know yet who need Jesus. We lift them up to Jesus in His name. Amen.

43

Mighty God, we lift up to You those in the news who make us mad, sad, or both. They need Jesus as much as we do. Please grant us a measure of Your patience and teach us to be gracious. Thank You for summer rains and our being able to see beauty around us. Forgive us for taking these gifts for granted. We love You Our Father, Our Savior, and the wondrous guidance and power of Your Spirit. Amen.

44

Heavenly Father, Your unrelenting love inspires us and humbles us. We fail You often and need another chance to be Your church that's needed in our community. Thank You for not giving up on us. Please increase our faith and fuel our passion to serve You Your way, for without You, we are nothing. We're Yours through Jesus Our Lord. Amen.

16

Merciful God, applause for You never seems quite enough, for our lives are energized by Your presence and power. We must come clean to say we don't deserve Your blessings. Thank You for the breath we have to say thank You, and for friends who encourage us. All of our hope is in You, Lord. Help us to hear the voices that remind us that we are accountable to You. We offer ourselves to You, just as we are through Jesus, our Savior. Amen.

46

Thank You for clear night skies when we can witness the vastness of Your creation, mighty God. We are filled with joy and praise for You. Forgive us when we seek guidance from friends and family before seeking You with prayer. Help us as a faith community to encourage and support one another through our difficulties. We surrender our worries to Your almighty hands in Jesus' name. Amen.

47

Magnificent and glorious God, we need to come together as a community to worship You, for we need Jesus' blood to wash away our sins. Thank You for the ears to hear Your message of hope loud and clear. Please let us take refuge in You when the media feed us painful messages. We lift up the sorrows and pains around us to You in Jesus' name. Amen.

48

Wondrously compassionate God, help us to be more courageous to confront wicked racism and gossip. We confess we're too often passive and fail to stand firm against these and other evils. You are all that is good, Lord, and Your blessings often amaze us. Thank You for providing us with the voices to make joyful noises to praise You. We cling to You with our desire to offer kindness and love to those suffering around us. In Jesus' name, Amen.

17

Loving Father in heaven, we praise You for providing us the ability to enjoy what we see, hear, taste, touch, and smell. Too easily we consume things in our world without pausing to appreciate these blessings from You. Thank You for the opportunities You give us to serve others in Your name. Please empower our efforts. We offer our hearts to You in Jesus' name. Amen.

50

In our community of faith, we are Yours and bound together with Your eternal love, Lord. Please help us to grow into our future as we make, mature, and multiply more faithful followers of Jesus. Thank You for generously providing for us to run this race of life until it is won. As Your unworthy servants, we praise and glorify You as we celebrate Jesus our Savior and pray in His name. Amen.

51

Timeless God, Our Father, we adore You. Thank You for renewing our hope in another day of possibilities with the gifts You provide to us. We, Your unworthy servants, hunger for a sense of Your presence and power, and to forgive us yet again. Please help us face our new challenges with a measure of Your creativity and joy, in Jesus name we pray, amen.

52

Incredibly gracious and loving God, despite our sins You keep surprising us with blessings. Thank You! Help us to be more faithful as we draw our strength and health from Your true vine, our Savior Jesus. As we seek the quiet time to be in His presence, may we be nourished by Your Holy Spirit and prepared to serve you ever more faithfully. It is in Jesus we pray. Amen.

18

Ever-present Father in heaven, we hunger for Your presence, for You have given us this beautiful life. We keep forgetting to thank You for the things we take for granted. Thank You for the sunrise of another day, a day of winter sunshine. Please strengthen us to stand together as a community of faith to serve You, in Your way. We are Yours through the power of Jesus' name. Amen.

54

Heavenly Father, Your creation is glorious, with sunlight dancing through green trees waving at blue skies. Our common sin is we often take for granted the goodness You provide. Thank You for not giving up on us and working to finish what You've started in us. Please keep showing us better ways to face the evils that assault us. We offer our best to You in Jesus' name. Amen.

55

Almighty Father, nothing is too difficult for You. We lift up to You our country's overwhelming problems, for too easily we can become part of them. Please help us to stay focused upon Your ways and purposes. Thank You for hearing our prayers, for the Deceiver can lead us astray without You. We know You deserve all the glory and praise as our victories are won through You. In the name of Jesus, Your Son, we pray. Amen.

56

Loving God, Your mercy and grace are amazing. In the wake of an ongoing crisis, we're even more aware of our sinful thoughts that betray us. Thank You for being so patient with us. As our world surrounds us with a fog of evil and uncertainty, please guide us and protect us as we feel our way into the future. We give our uncertainties and cares to You, in the name of Jesus, our Lord and Savior. Amen.

Eternal Father, You know us better than we know ourselves, yet You are merciful, gracious, and loving. Thank You for providing for us to be forgiven through Jesus' death on the cross. Furthermore, thank You for being our fortress against evil and our deliverer. Please continue to guide our community of faith and multiplying our efforts. We offer all that we are to You in Jesus' name. Amen.

58

Loving heavenly Father, in the midst of our wonderful country that You nourish so beautifully, vast numbers of our people are polarized with prejudices. Thank You for being our shield and fortress. Please show us ways You can use us to bring healing and peace to the communities around us. Use us for Your glory, we ask in Jesus' name. Amen.

59

Almighty God, all that we are and have are Yours. We ask that You help us to move in mission more effectively to our community. Thank You for hearing our prayers and responding in Your faultless way with Your perfect timing. Please forgive our often-clumsy efforts to serve You. All glory, honor, and praise belong to You through our Lord and Savior, Jesus, Amen.

60

Lord Jesus, we love You. We're sorry we don't spend more time seeking You, but instead we wait until it is convenient. Thank You for waiting, and for being so patient with us. We're told day by day that an invisible enemy is nearby to infect us. Keep reminding us that we have an unseen enemy who wants to separate us from You. We surrender to Your protection and loving care, Lord Jesus, in Your name. Amen.

We praise You, Lord, for You are the source of all of our blessings, none of which we deserve. Your mercy surpasses all of our sins. Thank You, gracious Lord. Our country is undeniably polarized. We ask for Your wisdom to determine what is true and right. Without You, we are nothing, but with You, everything is possible. We're humbled by the power in Jesus' name as we pray. Amen.

62

Lord Jesus, our Savior, have mercy on us. Your Word says You make all things new, so we ask You to help us start fresh as we move ahead. Thank You for redeeming us from so much wickedness. We find our rest, our joy, and all that is good in You. We sin against You unintentionally, and we need the power of Your shed blood to save us. To You, Jesus, belongs all praise, glory, and honor. Amen.

63

All-knowing and glorious God, there's no corner so dark You do not see, and there's no whisper so soft You cannot hear. Our secret sins can't be hidden from You. Forgive us, Lord, and thank You for saving us from ourselves. We often worry about our health and the health of those we love, so we submit to Your healing and redemption. It is in the name of Jesus, Your Son, and our Savior that we pray. Amen.

64

Gracious God, we praise You for providing our Prince of Peace, who is so welcome to live within us. Our hearts break when we see both injustice and evil rage. Forgive us for taking Your peace for granted, and we thank You for delivering us and forgiving us. Please let there be peace again in our country, and let it begin here with us. Use us, we pray for Your glory through Jesus, Amen.

Heavenly Father, when we thirst for You, we find Your Living Water, Jesus, and we praise You for His presence. We need Your salvation in Jesus' blood that was shed for us. Thank You for more chances to be like Him. Help us to be kind like Jesus in the midst of difficult people. They challenge us to live out our faith and share the gospel with them honestly. We're Yours through Jesus. Amen.

66

Amazing God, we praise You for binding us to Yourself and to each other with Your love. Thank You for letting Jesus' love flow so freely among us. It makes it easier to forgive each other as You have forgiven us. Please help us to learn from these recent days, and to prepare wisely for what lies ahead. Our future is in Your almighty hands. Amen.

67

Today's impossible tasks challenge us to see through Your eyes, mighty heavenly Father. In partnership with You through prayer, we know that wondrous things can and often do happen. Please forgive us for not trusting in You more. Thank You for leading us and protecting us during difficult days. Please increase our faith, for we depend upon You. We pray in Jesus' mighty name. Amen.

68

Holy God, what You give us to say or do is often met with skepticism or hostility. We can't run away from our responsibility as Jonah did, but we confess we're tempted. Thank You for Your patience, and please continue to show us Your ways through Jesus' life, as we make, mature, and multiply more of Jesus' faithful disciples. We offer ourselves and our spiritual community to You in His name. Amen.

Wondrous God, we worship You. Forgive us when we idolize people we know or things we have, cutting ourselves off from You. Thank You for providing for our every real need. Please help us let go of past successes and failures and move into the future with our Savior. We submit ourselves and our prayers to You in Jesus' name and for His glory. Amen.

70

Eternal God our Father, we know You lovingly hear our prayers, but so often we pray when full of doubt. Thank You for hearing us anyway. Please help our unbelief and teach us to pray with fewer doubts and greater faith in You. Use us and work through us, for we offer our hearts to You. It is there that we find greater strength to serve You and follow Your Son. In Jesus' name we pray. Amen.

71

We praise You, Father, for new life and fresh opportunities. Forgive us for focusing on our feet instead of looking ahead and to You. Thank You for Your new mercies and grace – sometimes we get discouraged. Grant that we may clearly see the path You've prepared for us, for Your way is always better. We offer our prayers through the power of Jesus' name. Amen.

72

We praise You, Lord, for Your unrelenting and forgiving love. We certainly don't deserve the blessings that are ours and couldn't possibly earn. Thank You for Your patience with us. Please help us to be the church You want us to be, despite those who want to restrict us, and please use us Your way. We surrender the challenges we face with prayer in Jesus' name. Amen.

23

Heavenly Father, You told David he would be King twenty years before it happened, and he waited. We confess we're often impatient with Your perfect timing. Thank You for teaching us to serve You on Your terms. Help us to be more faith-filled with our Savior, for we are His. We praise You for all the glories of Your creation around us as we pray in Jesus' name. Amen.

74

We offer our hearts to You, O Lord, because You alone are our fortress, delivering us from evil. Please teach us to bring healing and redemption to those in need. Thank You for using us for Your glory. We're sorry we don't seek Your presence and power more throughout each day. May Your praise always be on our lips, Father, in the name of Jesus, and in the power of Your Holy Spirit we pray. Amen.

75

Heavenly Father, when our prayers are answered, it makes You seem even more glorious. Forgive us when we don't step out in faith with You. Thank You for the experiences that lead us to trust You more. Please let us lean on You as we take uncertain steps into our future, hoping that we're not making mistakes. Our fears and worries we put into Your hands, in the name of Jesus. Amen.

76

Beautiful Savior, we belong to You, including all that we are. We need Your help to empower us as we serve our community. Thank You for challenging us with fresh opportunities to share the good news. Forgive us for clinging so stubbornly to our past ways of serving You. We love and adore You, heavenly Father, because of Jesus, Your only-begotten Son, and in His name we pray. Amen.

24

We join the heavenly chorus of angels in singing Your praises, Father. Thank You blessing us despite our stumbling and shortcomings. Even when we screw up, You show Your love for us. Please help us bring Your healing and grace to the many we know who need You. Our hearts are Yours, Father, because of Jesus within us, and we pray in His name. Amen.

78

Our faith in You, Heavenly Father, is not casual or drip-dry. We love those moments of worship when we can celebrate and enjoy Your presence. Thank You. Forgive us for those times when You reveal things to us, but we don't notice until later. Protect us, Lord of All, as we see our culture's foundations seem to be shaking. We surrender it all to You in and pray in the power of Jesus' name. Amen.

79

We are Yours, Lord Jesus, for in You our deepest needs are satisfied. We're reeling from recent weeks and months, so we ask for Your healing and redemption. Thank You for seeing us through the threats of evil. We confess we've feared the worst. Your glory has shown a light into our darkness, putting praise on our lips for You, our Creator, our Savior Jesus, and Your Holy Spirit. Amen.

80

We bask in the glory of Your gracious love, Father. We need Jesus' blood to cleanse us day by day. Thank You for delivering us from evil threats, both visible and invisible. Keep prompting us to share the good news with those who are lost in our community. You have called us to serve You for them, and we gladly obey, empowered by the power of Jesus' name. Amen.

Before we were conceived, Father, You had plans and a purpose for each of us, so we follow Jesus. Please keep our eyes and ears clear to stay on the path You've prepared for us. Thank You for helping us keep our heads held high as we walk through the storms of our lives. We're sad when we doubt Your faithfulness even while we are faithless. We praise You for all that You are – Creator, Son, and Holy Spirit. Amen.

82

Father, You continue to amaze us with the glories of Your creation, standing out in the midst of man-made messes. We're sorry that too often we don't see Your gifts of life amidst our pains and struggles. Thank You for making things new and fresh. Please keep reminding us that You're with us in our storms and battles. We surrender our worries and fears to You in Jesus' name. Amen.

83

When a media personality tells a lie about You, our Savior and Lord, all we can do is give them to You. Please help us respond to verbal and other attacks as You did to those that hated You. Thank You for providing us with our model and example to follow. We know we're not worthy to serve You, yet You love us and call us to serve You anyway. We praise You in Jesus' name. Amen.

84

Whether in the heat of summer or the frost of winter, Lord, You provide glorious and amazing life for us. We're sorry we complain so easily while Your blessings are abundant. Thank You. As we move forward into the future You have prepared for us, please help us stay focused upon You. Our hearts are Yours because You have provided our salvation through Jesus. Amen.

We can face anything today, Lord Jesus, because You are our strength. Yesterday's worries no longer matter, and tomorrow is in Your hands. To our shame, we never quite trust You enough. Thank You for our countless second chances to serve You more faithfully. Please help us to continue growing in our faith in You. Our lives are in You, our Lord Jesus, and in Your name we pray. Amen.

86

We give praise and glory to the Holy Spirit that guides and empowers us. With that power moving us, our faith grows stronger as we face our doubts. Thank You for not giving up on us and being patient. Please help us make, mature, and multiply more faithful followers of Jesus, for by His authority we grow His church, and in His name we pray. Amen.

87

Heavenly Father, we praise You with new songs in our mouths. Forgive us when we focus on our struggles and don't thank You for our blessings. Thank You for being our fortress amidst the storms of life. As we move ahead, we know we cannot return to the past, so help us find new ways to serve You and give You glory. We give You all that we are in response to Your calls upon us, giving us life in Jesus. Amen.

88

Glorious and humbling God, we offer our hearts to You because You give us so much. Save us from trying to restore previous plans and habits in our past and show us Your ways into our future as a community of faith. Thank You for past saints who have prepared our way. Our present shortcomings betray us. Yours is the power, glory, and majesty of Your Holy Trinity. Amen.

Glory and praise come from our voices, Lord, as You continue to be merciful despite our sins and shortcomings. Thank You for supplying us with more possibilities for renewed life when we think we're almost out. Help us to make the most of what we have as we show others Your salvation, love, and grace. In Jesus' name we praise You, Amen.

90

We offer our hearts to You, Lord, that we may be faithful. Help us, Lord, to be more effective and productive at making faithful disciples of our Savior, Jesus. Thank You for the opportunities You're giving us for making new friends who we can lead to Him. We're sorry we've ignored some of these chances in the past. We love You and praise You in the name of Jesus, Our Savior. Amen.

91

Our songs of praise come from our love for You, Lord Jesus. We know that Your shed blood cleanses us from our daily sins. Thank You for leading us into life worth living. We ask that You show us the best ways reach souls who are lost and help grow those who are learning to follow You. Your ways are better than ours, and we pray in Your name. Amen.

92

We praise You, heavenly Father, for better or worse, in sickness and in health, and to love and to cherish You here on Earth until we go home with Your Son, Jesus. We know we're sinners, forgiven through His blood. Thank You for loving us despite ourselves. Please show us how to meet today's challenges to make faithful disciples Your way, to mature by our faith in You, and to multiply more followers of Jesus, for it is in His name we pray, Amen.

Oh Jesus, we're not just Your fans: We're Your followers and are trying to be like You. Help us to live out the lingering crisis of our world triumphantly, as we walk with You and lead others towards eternal life with You. Thank You for sustaining us. Forgive us when we doubt you are leading us. To You belongs all praise and glory in Jesus' name. Amen.

94

Amazing God, we look outside and love seeing the glories of Your creation. Forgive us, for we give too little time and effort to who we are in the midst of others, while being and doing for others. Thank You for giving us time to slow down and engage in our community. Please help us help fulfill the needs of those around us. Our hearts are still offered to You through the power of Jesus' name. Amen.

95

Heavenly father, it is amazing when we pause to listen to You in silence, being totally still, we know Your presence and power. Thank You. Forgive us when we fill our lives with more and more things to do while emptying our lives of meaning and separating ourselves from others. Help us to be completely Yours, and use us for Your glory, we ask in Jesus' name. Amen.

96

We are Yours, Lord, all that we are and have. Please show us more effective ways to fulfill Your mission You have given us to our community around us. Thank You for delivering us from the evils that so often plague where we live. We don't deserve Your blessings and patience, as we continue to be sinners. We love You, Father, and we honor and praise You through Your Son, Jesus. Amen.

All-powerful and knowing God, we're always amazed by Your loving presence. We serve You and share the gospel, but we too easily fail You. We're often deceived by lying voices among those giving us "facts." Please grant us a measure of Your wisdom to discern how we must respond as a community of faith. We thank You, and we offer ourselves with our prayers in the name of Jesus. Amen.

98

Eternal God Our Father, we adore You. Our shortcomings betray us, even as we humble ourselves before You. Thank You for another day in which we can both serve You and serve others in the power of Jesus' name. Please keep our hearts sound, our lives pure, our thinking straight, and our spirits humble, as we surrender to Your forgiving presence and pray through Jesus' name. Amen.

99

Gracious God and heavenly Father, we can praise You no matter what happens. We put on a good front before friends and family, but we cannot hide anything from You. Thank You for loving us despite ourselves. Please increase our faith that we may serve You more effectively. Help us to keep walking and not faint, as we serve You Your way. We humbly offer our prayer in Jesus, Amen.

100

Despite the challenges we face, we catch glimpses of Your glory, so we love and bless You, O God. Through Jesus' blood, we know we're forgiven of our sins. We embrace Your mercy and kindness. Thank You for nudging us onto our current path. Please guide our feet to keep following You into our future, we pray. We truly belong to Our Creator, His Son, and Your Holy Spirit. Amen.

It is excellent to be still and know Your presence and power, Lord God. We love knowing You're with us when You speak through what You do in our lives. We're sorry we often miss seeing what You are doing. Thank You. Please help us to serve You better when things seem chaotic, for we hunger to see You glorified. We surrender our prayers in Jesus' name. Amen.

102

Gracious Father, the youngest apostle of Jesus says You are love, and we love You. Even though we're sinners, Your divine love flows steadily and dependably as You forgive us. Saying thank You hardly seems enough. Help us to be kind and loving towards those outside our church, including those hard to love, and help us lead them to Jesus. Use us as we follow the lead of Your Son we pray. Amen.

103

Thank You, glorious God, for binding us to one another with Your eternal love. We're Yours as a community of faith. Grant us the wisdom to discern facts amidst opinions as we face each of evil's challenges. We often get overwhelmed with life's daily things, and we've learned it is worth the effort to seek You first and pray in Jesus' name. Amen.

104

Father God of all good, we're tempted to worry about what this day may hold. We love You and love the freedom that's ours as we walk by faith in You. Thank You for the vision to see where You're leading us. Whether this is just another day of serving You or our last day, help us to make the most of this opportunity. We offer our prayer in Jesus' name. Amen.

Eternal God, we often worry when a dream You've given us isn't fulfilled quickly. Still, we adore placing our trust in You and Your divine timing. Thank You for giving our faith community the vision to perceive Your will and the ever-increasing faith to trust in You. Please help us to unite our individual gifts to serve You as one, as we offer ourselves to You through the power of Jesus' name. Amen.

106

Mighty Father, after conquering Jericho, one man's greed disabled Your people. We love being faithful to You because of Your divine faithfulness. Thank You for being forgiving and patient towards us. Please bring us together with others that need to know Our Savior, Jesus, and put what needs to be said to them on our lips. We offer our prayers for them and ourselves in Jesus' name. Amen.

107

Forgiving Father, even though Jesus is in our hearts, sometimes our pasts seem to haunt us. We love knowing that we're forgiven in Our Savior's blood, and we love being His. Thank You for crafting our futures and being our fortress against evils that surround us. Keep reminding us that the Enemy of our souls still tries to deceive us. We offer ourselves with our prayers in Jesus' name. Amen.

108

Caring and kind God, our coins say we trust You, but we often don't show it. Your caring patience with us moves us to love You more and more. Thank You for giving us additional second chances. As the community around our spiritual community struggles against evil, please multiply our efforts to serve them as we share the good news of Jesus, our Savior, in whose name we pray. Amen.

Forgive us, Heavenly Father, when we fail to focus on the plans and purposes You have for of us. We love how You have so amazingly equipped us to serve You Your way. Thank You for how You provide for us even as You deliver us from evils around us. Help us to focus clearly on the plans You have for us and to fulfill our purposes. We belong to Jesus and pray in His name. Amen.

110

Sometimes, precious Lord, we foolishly think we're alone in our battles against evil. We adore You passionately when we pause simply to be present to Your presence and power. Thank You for those opportunities to escape all distractions and enjoy Your presence. Please redeem and restore us when we remain in Jesus' vine. We offer ourselves again in service to You in His name. Amen.

111

O God, we thoughtlessly pursue perfection in ourselves when You simply ask us to pursue Jesus' holiness. We love Your helping us to pick up the pieces of our broken dreams and show us Your better way. Thank You for patiently turning our eyes back upon Jesus. Help us to remember service be about serving You, not about us. All we are and have we offer to You in Jesus' name. Amen.

112

Gracious God, we offer ourselves to serve You because You are already at work in our lives. Please help each of us to do our part to fulfill Your plans for our community of faith. Too easily we shift our focus from You to ourselves and our own needs. We love how You use us for Your good purposes to help other people in our community. We thank You, pray, and praise You in the name of Your Son, Jesus, our Savior. Amen.

Precious Lord Jesus, we are Yours because You have set us totally free. Please work through us and in us as You set others free from their bondage to the Father of Lies. Thank You for using us as a community of faith to share the gospel with others as we encourage one another. We're so easily enslaved to our past, and we praise and glorify You, and the Father, and the Holy Spirit as we pray. Amen.

114

Forgive us, Lord God, for we fail You so often, while You are patient and kind, and Your love never fails. Thank You for all the times You have shown us new and fresh ways to be Your church. As we are confronted with a new world of challenges, please shed Your light into the darkness to reveal the path You've prepared for us. In the power of Jesus' name, we live and pray. Amen.

115

We offer our best efforts, Heavenly Father, as we accept these new challenges for Your church. Please empower and guide us to fulfill the dreams You've given us and sow the seeds of Your gospel. Thank You for the opportunities to bless our community with the fulfillment of those dreams. We're sorry we doubted it could be done. We give You glory and love in Jesus' name. Amen.

116

Holy Lord God, we often sing Your praises, and we declare our love for Jesus. We too often confuse dreams for ourselves with Your plans for us. After a crisis, we're so thankful for having a new beginning, and sometimes a new path. As we focus upon You, please grant us the vision to perceive Your will, and increase our faith to believe in the dream You've given us. We offer our prayer in Jesus. Amen.

Knowing our weaknesses, Lord Jesus, we give ourselves to You. Help us, O Lord, to face our hidden prejudices and find unity in Your cross as our equalizer. Thank You for showing us how to love people just as they are. The media seem to expect us to hate those who are different than we are. We worship You and bless You as we lift up our prayers in the name of Jesus. Amen.

118

We have sometimes prayed as though giving You orders, O Lord. Forgive us. We're in awe of You and of Your love, and we love being present to Your presence. Thank You for being ready to listen to our prayers even before we pray. Please strengthen us emotionally and spiritually as we walk with our Master and Savior, Jesus. We offer our prayers in His name. Amen.

119

We offer to serve You Your way, Heavenly Father. Please continue to be patient and kind towards us, even when we go astray from what Jesus teaches us. We want to focus upon following our Savior who is leading us and empowering us. We thank Jesus and love Him so much because He first showed his love for us in His life, death, and resurrection. It is in His precious name we pray.

120

Only You, Yahweh, are our amazingly gracious God, and our beloved Jesus is our King. We're sinners, but we're forgiven because our King died for us. Thank You, Lord, for making us Yours when we've accepted You as our Savior. Please guide us through our new world with its new challenges and show us Your plans for us. We offer You our devotion and our prayers in Jesus' name. Amen.

We surrender to Your mercy and grace, Almighty God. As we study Your Word and worship You, please open our eyes to see Your light shining into our darkness. Thank You for showing us that Your grace is not just a concept, but the reality of who You are for us. We confess our doubts sometimes hold us back from seeing You glorified in our efforts to serve. That glory and praise belong to You. Amen.

122

Eternal God, Our Father, our hearts are Yours because all things are possible with You. Show us how to function as a family united in Your love. Thank You for fresh life each morning and giving us greater faith growing out of our previous doubts. We strive for a measure of Jesus' holiness as we follow Him. It is in the power of His name that we pray. Amen.

123

We offer You as we are, heavenly Father. Since You hold the future, we ask that You guide our often-uncertain steps amidst the voices telling us what we cannot do. Such evil often makes us fearful though we depend upon You. We adore our Savior and King, who guides us into eternity. Thank You for sending Jesus to live, die, and rise from the dead for us, and it is in His powerful name we pray. Amen.

124

Infinitely powerful God, You have many reasons to judge us, so we praise You for sending Jesus to pay debts to You. We know our sin and try to please You, but we still stumble. Thank You for generously and tolerantly guiding us towards the holiness of Jesus. Bless our governments' leaders to do what is right and not just what's expedient. We surrender to You in Jesus' holy name. Amen.

Forgiving Father, our sins and shortcomings still stain our lives with evil. We praise You for looking beyond our sins because of Your love. Thank You for helping us thrive professionally and personally because of Your grace. Please let Jesus dwelling in our hearts empower us with strength and wisdom as we walk with Him into the future. We surrender and offer our prayers in His name. Amen.

126

Gracious good Father, please continue to put Your Holy Word on our lips and tasks to do Your way. We are Yours. Some of us are always receptive and encouraging of others in our church family, but a few are not. Thank You for determining our path as a church and being our shield and fortress. Forgive our fear, for we praise and adore Our Father, Savior, and Holy Spirit. Amen.

127

When life seems like hell, O God, worship and prayer bring us a touch of heaven because we are Yours. Please challenge us with new ways to be Your church. Thank You for calling us into Your family. We're still sinners who need Christ's blood to cleanse us and redeem us. We love You and worship You in the name of Your only begotten son, Jesus, and pray in His Holy name. Amen.

128

Holy Lord God, You are gloriously wise and eternal. Please forgive our idolatry from worshipping ourselves, our possessions, and our accomplishments. Thank You for giving us more chances to serve You, be Yours, and thrive. Help us to look beyond the sources of lies to see Your truth, Your ways, and Your abundant life. We offer our prayers in Jesus' glorious name. Amen.

Even if we don't witness a miracle today, Lord, we are Yours. We ask for opportunities today to lead people to Our Savior as we contribute to our spiritual community and beyond. Thank You for hearing our prayers, even when we don't see Your answers. We confess our hope that You'll serve us rather than vice versa. We praise and love You, heavenly Father, in Jesus' name. Amen.

130

We confess we tend to worry as we face our current challenges rather than see it all as tests of our faith in You, gracious God. We love You and need to trust You more. Thank You for supplying all of our real needs. Please help us understand how You want us to face our challenges and respond in faith. All that we have, and all our efforts are for You, for it is in the power of Jesus' name we pray. Amen.

131

We dedicate our time, talent, training, and resources to You, our amazing God. We ask that You be with us as we face today's evils, just as You were with Your chosen people as they entered their promised land. Thank You for being our warrior companion. We regret our worries in light of Your faithfulness. We give You all the glory and honor as we offer our prayer in Jesus' name. Amen.

132

Precious Lord Jesus, we're following You and living courageously and cheerfully, despite our difficulties, because we trust in what we don't see yet from You. We admit we're sometimes fearful anyway. Thank You for Your faithfulness. Increase our faith, that we may serve You more effectively, as we make, mature, and multiply more faithful disciples of Jesus. In His name we pray. Amen.

We offer our prayers, Lord Jesus, because they are essential to our partnership with You. Help us to be one in Your Spirit and one in Your love as You binds us to Yourself and each other. Forgive our sometimes-shaky faith. We love Your always standing by us as a community of our faith in You. We offer heartfelt thanks and praise in Your name. Amen.

134

We confess, almighty God, we've greedily asked too often for things we don't really need. We love the abundant life You have provided. Thank You. Please show us how we can more effectively share the gospel and more generously share the abundance with which You have surrounded us. We offer ourselves to You, that You may use us for Your glory, and for the glory of Jesus. In His name we pray. Amen.

135

We trust in You, Heavenly Father. We ask You to reveal to us what You are doing out of Your goodness for our community that Your kingdom may come and be fully manifested. Thank You for being our shield. We know we're still sinners, yet we're forgiven because of Jesus shedding His blood for us. We love You, our Heavenly Father, Your Son Jesus, and Your Holy Spirit empowering us. Amen.

136

Almighty, eternal, and all-knowing heavenly Father, knowing You are real fills us with awe. Though we try to be like Your Son, Jesus, we fail miserably. Thank You for sending Him to give us Your way, truth, and life. Help us to teach others to seek You as we share the gospel in a language they can understand and embrace. All our efforts are consecrated to You and Jesus. In His name we pray. Amen.

We surrender to Your perfect timing. O God. Help us show others that now is the perfect time to start following Jesus and join us joyfully to do so. Forgive our sometimes-sour attitudes, even though we know we're Yours. We love serving You and worshiping You. We know that compared to the suffering of others, we live a life of blessing. We offer our thankful prayer in Jesus' name. Amen.

138

We're often scared of trying new things, Lord. We love You and want to have the courage to trust You, but our faith is often weak. Thank You for reassuring us in the Bible that all things are possible with You. Grant us the eyes to recognize Your will and the heart to comprehend Your still small voice as You lead us. We offer ourselves just as we are, and we pray in Jesus' name. Amen.

139

Awesome God, we praise You as You bless us. Jesus calls us to be willing to risk everything for Him, but we easily evade that responsibility. Thank You for drawing us into the cause of Christ. Increase our faith and our courage, O God, for we know that what we gain in following Jesus will endure forever. We choose to surrender the earthly things we hold dear in the name of Jesus. Amen.

140

We submit ourselves to serve You, O Lord of our hopes and future. Please, O God, equip us to accomplish what You are calling us to do, which is far more than we imagined. We admit we are somewhat apprehensive. Thank You for keeping us on the path You have divinely prepared for us. We're also prepared to glorify Your name as we worship You and pray in Jesus' name. Amen.

We're letting go of our pride, Heavenly Father. As we move ahead as Your church, help us live with mutual decisions and not be pushy. We share in Your unconditional love. Thank You for the leadership we have from Jesus. Our love for one another as we follow Him is sometimes clumsy. We love experiencing Your divine presence as we worship You and pray in Jesus' name. Amen.

142

God of limitless possibilities, You are amazing. We tend to cling to the past instead of trusting You with our future. Thank You for being so patient and loving towards us despite our shortcomings. Please show us Your way to adjust to the changes in our culture. We lift up our questions with our prayers in Jesus' name. Amen.

143

Righteous heavenly Father, we are trying to embrace the new pathway You are revealing to us because it seems You've prepared us for it. We admit we're still intimidated by so much behind us. Please increase our courage and strengthen our faith in You. You are our fortress, and we love Your standing with us. We thank You and praise You in the power of Jesus' name. Amen.

144

Lord Jesus, sometimes it is awfully hard to stay focused on You, as we are so easily distracted. We love You and love all that You have done, filling us with joy, peace, patience, kindness, goodness, faithfulness, gentleness, and self-control. Thank You. We remember how You ordered the stormy sea to calm down, and we ask for a measure of Your divine peace. We offer our prayer in Your name. Amen.

We serve You Your way, Lord God, as You called us. We ask that You help us cope with attacks on Christianity and Your church. Thank You for being our Rock on which You have built Your church. Forgive us when we are afraid instead of trusting You. You are gloriously our Savior, best friend, and always-present God. Amen.

146

When we find quiet with no distractions, we love enjoying Your presence and power, heavenly Father. We are awed and speechless, just as in heaven when the Lamb opened the seventh seal. Forgive us when we begin making demands before humbling ourselves before You. Teach us to pray while in Jesus' name. We humbly offer this request in the power of that name. Amen.

147

We offer You our allegiance, gracious God. We ask for Your help in becoming more like Your Son, Jesus. We know we're sinners, but we're cleansed by His blood shed for us to cleanse us. We love communing with our glorious God in prayer. We're careful what we pray for because You are so graciously willing to answer. We're thankful and humbled by Your constant holy presence. Amen.

148

Facing our sins, Lord Jesus, we're embarrassed. Your eternal forgiving love is but one aspect of Your amazing grace. Thank You for delivering us from evil and equipping us generously to sow the seeds of the gospel and serve our community. Please help us finish what You've started in us and don't give up on us. We surrender our clumsy efforts to Your guidance through Jesus. Amen.

Heavenly Father, we love You because You first have shown Your love for us. We try to avoid sinning against You, but we do so anyway, and we fail to serve You as effectively as we intend to. Thank You for patiently forgiving us. Please protect us as we witness injustice around us more frequently even while we're battling evil for others. We offer our prayers in Jesus' name. Amen.

150

We offer our hearts as well as our efforts, gracious God. Please help us extend Your divine love with our friendship as we share the gospel with others. People often need so much more than our friendship. Thank You for providing opportunities to serve You this way. We confess that some of our best intentions have unintended consequences. We worship and adore You in Jesus. Amen.

151

Forgive us, eternal God, when our prayers are limited to half-hearted thanksgivings followed by requests. Your unwavering patient love is utterly amazing. Thank You for blessing us far more than we could possibly deserve, let alone earn. Please help us discern what You ask of us beyond our selfish agenda for our family and friends and recognize other needs beyond us. Use us, we ask in the name of Jesus, our Savior and Lord of our Lives. Amen.

152

All glory, praise, and honor are justly Yours, loving Father. Forgive us our shortcomings, we pray, and wash the stain of sin off us with Jesus' blood. Thank You for the eyes to see and ears to hear how You are at work among us. Please multiply our efforts to serve the community around us and spread the good news of our Savior, Jesus. We offer our prayers in Jesus' holy and powerful name. Amen.

We surrender to Your mercy and grace, Lord Jesus. Help us help our neighbors in the community around our church, for they need kindness and patience from us, as well as forgiveness and encouragement. We have often failed them, unintentionally. Our hearts are filled with love for You as we worship and praise You. Thank You for saving us for Your good purposes, for Your glory, and for the glory of our creator Father. Amen.

154

Forgive us, Our Father, when we abuse the freedom we have through Jesus, our Savior. We give praise to Your Holy Spirit that guides and empowers us, while Jesus saves us. Thank You. As You explained to Jeremiah, heavenly Father, before we were conceived You knew us and had plans and a purpose for each of us. Please keep pointing us towards Your purposes and plans for us. We offer our prayers in Jesus' powerful name. Amen.

155

We surrender to Your power and truth, Lord Jesus. Please guide us with Your truth and lead us Your way in Your life. Thank You for the vision to perceive the will of our God, for the faith to believe in what You reveal to us, and for the courage we need to fully trust You. We're not yet where You want us to be. We love You for saving us despite ourselves. We pray in Your name. Amen.

156

We hunger for You, gracious God. Help us to thrive in You as we're empowered to serve You by Your Holy Spirit. Forgive us for not showing more love for You through telling others of Your presence and power. We love singing Your praises when we gather as a church to hear Your Word preached and to pray. Thank You for the freedom we have to be Yours and serve in Jesus' name. Amen.

Forgive us, O God, when we fail to brag about You when things don't seem to be going well enough. All our hope is in You, and we want to praise and love You at all times. Thank You for our call to sow the seed of the gospel and offer Your healing love to our neighbors. Help us to be real and honest as we exercise and share our faith. We offer our prayer in Jesus' holy name. Amen.

158

We're sorry, Lord, when we sometimes fail to trust You completely with what is best. We love reminding each other of Your goodness when we worship You together. Thank You for binding us together with Your perfect love. Please glorify Yourself as You magnify our puny efforts to serve You and share the gospel. We're nothing without our God and King. We pray in Jesus' name. Amen.

159

We're humbled, heavenly Father, when You reveal love, beauty, and honor in the midst of our messy world. Keep reminding us that love is more than feelings, beauty is beyond appearance, and honor goes deeper than opinions describing ourselves. Thank You for giving us measures of Your wisdom to see Your truth as we proceed along the path where You clear away the rubble of life. We're sorry when we see the rubble without seeing You. We worship and adore You in Jesus' name. Amen.

160

Awesome God, we offer this prayer now because we anticipate what You are accomplishing. Since You've given us the good seed of the gospel, please help us sow Your seed in hearts that are ready to receive Jesus, our Savior, that Your church may have a bountiful harvest. Our past efforts can be much more effective. We love being present to Your presence. With thanks we pray in Jesus. Amen.

We're sorry, Lord Jesus, that it is easier to share our heavenly Father's love with focus on Your manger than on Your empty tomb. We love holding You in our hearts in worship. Thank You for each opportunity we have to sing Your praises. Please help us be better agents of joy for both the manger and the empty tomb. We offer our hearts in prayer to You in Your name. Amen.

162

We humble ourselves before You, gracious God, and ask that You grant us the vision to perceive Your holy will, for increased faith to believe in all You reveal to us, and for greater courage to trust in You in all things. Thank You for Your faithful love. Forgive us for not being more faithful to You. Together we sing Your praises in public worship, and our praise continues in our hearts every day. Amen.

163

Amazing God, we love how Your light shines into the darkness of our lives. Too often we let evil's darkness overcome us. Thank You for empowering us to share the blessings of Your Holy Presence along with the good news. Help us to have our eyes open to more effective ways of communicating Your love to those suffering so much from the challenges of our present time. We surrender all that we are and have to You in Jesus' name. Amen.

164

Daily Bible reading confronts our sinful nature, O God. We hunger to know You more fully and praise all that You do in our lives. Thank You for Your faithful, loving care. Please use Your Word working through us like spiritual sandpaper, smoothing our rough edges and polishing larger areas of our lives. We are Yours, and we live and pray in the power of Jesus' name. Amen.

We submit to Your divine authority, Lord. Please help our church make the best use of both our gifts and our limitations, so we may be good stewards. Thank You for providing us the sense not to challenge either our limitations or Your limitless power and grace. Too easily we forget that with You all things are possible. We praise, thank, and love You as we pray in Jesus' name. Amen.

166

We worship Your presence and holiness, heavenly Father. Forgive us when we want discipline and rigid standards for others and mercy for ourselves. Thank You for Your patience and grace. Help us pursue Your mercy and justice for all as we do ministries and share the gospel. We humbly offer our prayer in the powerful name of Jesus. Amen.

167

We lay our lives at Your feet, Lord Jesus and give You all that we are. Show us, Lord, the battles with evil worth fighting, and please deliver us from other conflicts. We are too easily distracted, Lord, with useless political battles. We love spending time with an awareness of Your presence with music and prayer, and we thank You for the privilege of serving You. We pray this in Your name. Amen.

168

Be glorified, through the beauty of Your world and in our serving You, Heavenly Father. Challenge us to dare boldly and venture into difficulties that show Your power in unfamiliar places, and where we find joy in You. Thank You for the eyes to see Your grace and forgive our anxiety. You are the truth that calls in quiet whispers and through storms, Lord, as we pray in Jesus' name. Amen.

Glorious and loving God, forgive us in those times when we consider ourselves to be helpless before the challenges we face. Thank You for being our strength when we feel weak. Please use us on Your terms, through Your way, for Your glory. Once again, we surrender all that we are and have. We pray in the power of Jesus' name. Amen.

170

Through our Savior Jesus and in no other name we offer ourselves to You, righteous heavenly Father. Push back the horizons of our dreams and hopes and push us into the future You've prepared for us. Forgive our ignorance and our self-reliance. We love You and the everyday blessings You provide. We thank You with and offer our prayer in Jesus' name. Amen.

171

Heavenly Father, forgive us when we have not thought for others and no cares but for ours. We love and worship You on Sundays anyway. We thank You for being alive and to sing Your praises in Jesus name. Teach us to forgive, as You forgive. We offer You our love and our prayer in Jesus' name. Amen.

172

Gracious God, we worship You and adore You. Forgive us when we take for granted all that You have done for us. We thank You for fighting the battles of our lives beside us. Give us new occasions to prompt us with new testimonies we may offer and more thanksgiving to You. We praise You in the midst of our trials, for You are indeed the reason why we are so happy. We offer our prayer in Jesus' name. Amen.

Magnificent God, we magnify Your name. Help us see Your path among conflicting voices around us. When life distracts us and our focus shifts, forgive us. Who feels the pain we endure and comforts us as You do with Your divine love? Father, we thank You because we know You will never leave us nor forsake us. We humbly pray in Jesus' name. Amen.

174

When we impose our own will over Yours, forgive us merciful Father in heaven. We adore You because You are our great provider and so much more. Lord, we thank You because You are bigger than all our problems, and You are our shield. Help us find lives that are lost and lead them to salvation in Jesus. In His Holy name we offer our prayer. Amen.

175

Lord Jesus, we humbly lift Your name higher above all other names, above every 'thing' else. Empower us to be Your people that bring Your love and the gospel to those who are lost. We thank You because You are our salvation. Forgive us when we are timid about sharing the gospel. We love You, our righteous Savior and God, and we pray through the power of Jesus' name. Amen.

176

We surrender ourselves to You, loving Father in heaven. Help us reach out to broken hearts and draw them into Your love. We are Your children who often fail to live in Your peace. Forgive us. We love how You hear the thoughts of our hearts. Thank You for being more ready to hear our prayers than we are to pray. We're Yours and we pray in Jesus' name. Amen.

Forgive us, Lord God, when You give us a word to say as Your voices and we are silent. Thank You for graciously forgiving us. Give us another chance O Lord, and we will boast of Your goodness, and of Your great kindness all day long, and we will praise You for being our God. We're still breathing, so we keep offering You our prayers in Jesus' name. Amen.

178

We surrender all to You: our lives, families, children, friends, career, finances, our prayers, our relationships. We surrender it all, Lord Jesus. We ask that You use us for Your glory Your way. We thank You for the grace of the lives we have with ours. Please keep forgiving our shortcomings. We praise and love You, and we pray in Jesus' name. Amen.

179

May our praise and love for You be pleasing to You, heavenly Father. We humbly come before Your throne and ask for forgiveness of our sins. Thank You for saving us from ourselves. We ask You to help us lead others in our community to salvation, to help their faith grow, and teach them to multiply faithful disciples. We surrender to You, our healer. In Jesus' name we pray. Amen.

180

Who hears us as we confess our sins and forgives as You do, Lord? We love You because of who You are, our good and Merciful Father. Thank You for everything, including all we too easily take for granted. Saturate our thoughts with Your presence so that we may be like You, think as You do, give as You do, but most of all, to love as You do. We offer our prayer in Jesus' name. Amen.

Father, we praise You, for we have won the victory in Christ Jesus. Take control of our thoughts. Rebuke the evil one from anything to do with our lives and those people in our lives. We thank You because the devil cannot stop us as we live in Jesus' name. Too easily we don't confront evil. Oh Lord, we praise You with music in Your house, the church, before the saints, in Jesus name. Amen.

182

Oh Lord, we sing aloud Your praises before unbelievers, and we are not ashamed. Search our hearts and minds of all inequities and strip us of all our unrighteousness, as we come to You just as we are. Thank You for Your continuing grace. Help us to encourage one another to grow in our faith. We surrender all we have and are to You in Jesus' name. Amen.

183

Your precious love in our lives, O God, is what we count most valuable. Let Your glory overwhelm our enemies, and may they scatter with fire as we walk on Your path. Sometimes we carelessly assume that there's no evil working against us. Father, we adore You, our deliverer and our salvation. We humbly offer our prayer in Jesus' name. Amen.

184

Oh Lord, we praise You, for You are good, and Your mercies endure forever. We pray everyone praying this prayer is blessed with the gift of Your Holy Spirit, that their lives will be led by Your will. Thank You for Your mercy and patience. Where can we go from Your Spirit? Where can we hide our sins from You? We love You because You are our God, and we're Yours in Jesus' name. Amen.

Father, we praise You and embrace You because of Your unwavering faithfulness in our lives. We're glad Your love sees our failings and forgives. Thank You. Grant Your great will to be done in our lives and the lives of our neighbors, and Yours will be the very thoughts and actions we carry out in order to please You. We offer our prayer in Jesus' name. Amen.

186

We humbly come before You with our prayers, heavenly Father. Please heal and help the sick. Sustain both their bodies and their spirits. Too often we have sided with the media, speaking discouragement. We praise You, Lord, for You are bigger than the biggest, stronger than the strongest, better than the best, and source of all that is loving and good. We thank You in Jesus' name. Amen.

187

Lord Jesus, You know our sins and understand our actions, and now we ask Your forgiveness. We love how You are always patient and consistently merciful to us. Thank You. Give the young and the strong the needed caution to keep them from unwittingly spreading disease and inspire them to help. We offer our prayer to You and in the power of Your name. Amen.

188

Beautiful, wonderful Creator of heaven and earth, we give You praise and all the glory. Forgive our secretive thoughts, and direct and rebuke us. We thank You for our lives that are ours because of Your grace. Dear God, protect our vulnerable neighbors around and within our church. Only You can do what no man or woman can do. We surrender our community to You in Jesus name. Amen.

May our praise and worship please You, O God. Provide for the poor, we pray, especially for the uninsured and homeless. For those days when we forget to seek Your presence and power, forgive us. We adore You and we want everyone to know about our lives in Your loving care. Thank You for all of our blessings. We ask in Jesus' name. Amen.

190

Forgive our selfish pride, Lord God in heaven, for we like to think we can depend upon ourselves and not You. Nothing is too difficult for You, our amazingly gracious God. Thank You for being so attentive to our needs. Lord, help our elected officials as they allocate the necessary resources when needed. All that we are, we surrender to Your divine care in Jesus' name. Amen.

191

We offer our devotion as we pray, O Lord. We pray for our scientific community leading the charge to understand diseases and afflictions. Give them knowledge, wisdom, and a persuasive voice of truth. Thank You for opening doors to discoveries. In Your mercy forgive our sinful ways. We love being in Your divine presence, singing Your praises, and offering our prayers in the power of Jesus' name. Amen.

192

Oh Lord, we join the cloud of witnesses in heaven who have gone before us and offer this prayer. O God, help the media to communicate with appropriate seriousness and accuracy. Forgive us when we accept the word of a source without double checking. By Your grace we are forgiven, and in Your peace our lives are fully lived. Thank You for hearing our prayer in Jesus' name. Amen.

When our praise and worship fail to please You, forgive us heavenly father. Let the music in our worship help us magnify and glorify You. Thank You for sustaining us with everyday blessings. Help us find the most helpful local information to equip us to be good neighbors who share the gospel and Your love. We lift up our neighbors to You in Jesus' name. Amen.

194

We love You, O Lord, for Your love sustains us and binds us together as a community of faith. Keep us from anxiety when facing our challenges, and enable us to implement Your strategies, even at a cost to ourselves. Thank You for defending and sustaining us. Forgive us when we don't seek You with enough prayer. We worship and adore You in Jesus' name. Amen.

195

Father God, we are holding nothing back, as we come before Your glorious throne with our love. O Lord, You have searched us and know our sins. Thank You for washing away the stains of our sin with Jesus' blood. For those with mental health challenges, who feel isolated, anxious, and helpless, Lord, provide them every necessary support. Let our prayers be offerings in Jesus' name. Amen.

196

We love and worship You, O Lord our God. Protect the homeless from disease and who are unable to practice the protocols of social distancing in the shelter system. If we can help, show us how. Thank You for our homes, friends, and families. Forgive us when we've seen needs and not responded. We love serving You, and we pray in Jesus' name. Amen.

We join everlasting music and praise in heaven for You, heavenly Father. We're ashamed of our sins and grateful we're forgiven. Lord God, provide Christian missionaries throughout the world with words of hope, and equip them to love and serve those around them. May our prayers serve to provide encouragement and protection. In the power of Jesus' name we pray. Amen.

198

You are an awesome God, and as You love us first, we love You. O God, there are workers facing layoffs and financial hardship. Inspire Your church to help where we can. Forgive us when we're uncertain how to respond even with Your help. Heavenly Father, the power in Your name is awesome. Thank You for sending Jesus and calling us together to celebrate his work. In his name, Amen.

199

Lord, in Your mercy change our hearts and minds so we function as Your special people. We love declaring that You are King of Kings and Lord of Lords. Thank You for being our Lord. For families with Young children at home for the foreseeable future, help us help parents, and to partner together creatively for the care and flourishing of their children. Help single parents, grow their networks of support. We offer our prayer in Jesus' name. Amen.

200

You alone are the God we love, Lord. We lift up parents to You who cannot stay home from work, but they must find care for their children. Please give them creative solutions. Forgive our selfish focus upon our own needs. You have made our hearts, so help us to love You more. Thank You for opportunities to share the gospel while we meet others' needs in Jesus' name. Amen.

Merciful God, we confess we have sinned against You in thought, word, and deed, but we love You with all our thoughts and prayers. Thank You for the forgiving and redeeming blood of Jesus. We pray for business leaders making decisions that affect the lives of their employees. Give these women and men some of Your wisdom. We offer ourselves to Your service in Jesus' name. Amen.

202

Glorious God, we offer our lives to You with praise and love. We pray for pastors and church leaders faced with the challenges of social distancing and ask You to help them to pastor their congregants and love their communities as well. Thank You. In Your mercy, forgive what we have been, and help us amend who we are. We worship You in Jesus' name. Amen.

203

Lord, You are eternal and all-powerful, yet You love to hear children praise You. We pray for students, whose courses of study are changing, placements are canceled, and graduations are uncertain. Help us help them know that while life is uncertain, they can trust You. We have failed to love You with our whole heart, mind, and strength, but we pray in Jesus' name. Amen.

204

Heavenly Father, You are awesome beyond our understanding. May Your Holy Spirit inspire us to pray, give, love, serve, and to proclaim the gospel, that Jesus might be glorified in our community. We have not loved our neighbors as ourselves, but direct what and who we shall be. You alone authentically love us and care for us, calling us to walk with You. Thank You in Jesus' name. Amen.

Eternal God, our judge and redeemer, we confess that we can't hide from You, for we have sinned. Your faithfulness goes right up past the sky. Thank You for always being available to us. Heavenly Father, keep health care workers and their families safe and healthy. We praise You for the love that is always ready to welcome us and bring us home in Jesus' name. Amen.

206

Lord God, we join together to declare Your praise. Help us to follow in the footsteps of our faithful shepherd, Jesus, who laid down his life for the sake of love. Thank You for Your grace. We confess we have too often lived for ourselves and turned from our neighbors. Heavenly Father, Your righteousness is bigger than our minds can fathom, and we worship You in Jesus' name. Amen.

207

Your justice is far deeper than the sea, glorious God. Lord, help health care workers to stay clear-minded, even when in the midst of the surrounding panic. Thank You for being our peace in the midst of chaos, our shelter from the storms of life. We confess we have at times refused to bear the troubles of others. Your grace and love are marvelous, and we pray in the power of Jesus' name. Amen.

208

Glorious God, we are Yours. Teach us how to glorify Jesus' name more effectively, and also equip us with everything we need. Merciful God, we confess that we have often failed to be an obedient church to do what You call us to do Your best way. We love serving You and making, maturing, and multiplying faithful followers of Jesus. We thank You for that privilege in His name. Amen.

Almighty and gracious God, mercifully forgive our sin and free us from selfishness. We love You, Father, and want to see You are here, learn more about You, and follow You alone. Thank You for letting us be aware of You. Please deliver doctors and their staffs from anxiety for their own aging parents, children, spouses, or roommates. We surrender our praise in Jesus' name. Amen.

210

You have blessed us to feel the morning wind on our faces and to sense Your presence, so we worship You. Teach us to be Your faithful people in a time of crisis. Thank You for graciously providing for us. We have not always done Your will, and we have rebelled against Your love. We, Your flawed people, worship You and pray in Jesus' name. Amen.

211

Holy Lord God almighty, we love You. Cleanse us from our sins, and please deliver us from proud thoughts. Thank You for faithfully delivering us from evil and from those who hate Your church. Merciful God, give nurses, doctors, and therapists compassion for every patient in their care. We worship You with music in our praise. We pray in Jesus' name. Amen.

212

Humbly we draw near, O God, confessing our faults, asking for Your mercy, and finding in You our refuge. We adore You. Thank You for listening to us, regardless of our age. Help Christians in health care to exhibit such peace, so many would ask about the reason for their hope and give them opportunities to proclaim the gospel. With them we will worship You in Jesus' name. Amen.

We can do nothing without You, Lord, but with You, all things are possible. Help us spread the gospel with Your divine love. Thank You for sustaining us and sustaining our efforts to witness for Jesus. We are often silent when we should speak, and useless when we could be useful. We worship You with every fiber of our being in Jesus' name. Amen.

214

Loving and merciful Father, we hide under Your wings and worship You so we can be safe, for everything that is alive relies on You. Forgive us and free us from our sins. Thank You for guiding us. Search us, O God, and know our hearts; test us and know our anxious thoughts as You lead us in Your everlasting way. We glorify You in Jesus' name. Amen.

215

Almighty and merciful God, You are faithful, and kind, and we humble ourselves before You. We ask that You provide for Your children financially, especially if they fall ill and are unable to work. We have often erred and strayed from Your ways like lost sheep. You are the source of all life, and in Your light, we see light. In Jesus' name. Amen.

216

Heavenly Father, we surrender all that we have and are to You. Please take away the roadblocks that stop us from coming into Your presence and fill in the potholes that slow us down, making the way bumpy. Thank You for Your faithfulness. We often follow too much the desires of our own hearts rather than You. We praise You and thank You in Jesus' name. Amen.

We worship You, Father, with prayers, Your Word, music, and witness. Spare those of us who confess our faults and restore those who are penitent. Thank You for Your mercy. Make us children of quietness and heirs of Your peace when we listen to Your silent voice as we pray. We're humbled by Your glorious presence as we pray in Jesus' name. Amen.

218

We humble ourselves, gracious God. We ask that we have unity amidst diversity, loving those in other spiritual communities where we have little in common but the gospel. Lord God, we know You love us, but we do not love You fully as we could. Our fulfillment is in loving and serving You. Thank You for all You provide, including everyday blessings. We pray in Jesus' name. Amen.

219

Merciful God, You call, but we do not always listen. We often walk away from neighbors in need, wrapped in our own concerns. There is no one like You, **Glorious Creator**, You make the wind blow and the rain fall, Thank You. We pray that church members would be good and do good in their workplaces this week. We worship You in Jesus' name. Amen.

220

Precious Lord Jesus, You are our only way, truth, and life for us. We are too easily blind to evil, hatred, and greed, believing it's not in our neighborhood. Forgive us and please open our eyes. Thank You for these opportunities. Lord, light the fire of Your love in our hearts for them and strengthen our weakness to witness to the gospel by Your power. We ask in Your name. Amen.

We want to see, hear, and know Your living presence, heavenly Father, for You are the Lord of our lives. We pray that a culture of discipling will form in which making disciples is viewed as an ordinary part of our Christian life. We humbly confess our sins and ask Your mercy. You are our glorious God. We offer our prayer in Jesus' name. Amen.

222

Merciful God, pardon all of us who truly repent and turn to You, we pray. We love You, for we are Yours. Thank You for always hearing our prayers. We pray more of us would use their careers to take the gospel to places it's never been, then use us to share the gospel. We surrender our lives to Your service for Your purposes. We pray in Jesus' name. Amen.

223

We hunger for You, Holy Spirit, so together we may celebrate Your glory. We pray that hopes for political change will be eclipsed by the hope of heaven. Thank You for using us to share the gospel. We have not loved You with a pure heart, nor have we loved our neighbor as ourselves. May Your work among us glorify You, we pray in Jesus' name. Amen.

224

We are humbled by the work of the Holy Spirit, and so offer glory and honor to our Savior, Jesus. Please help church members share the gospel this week and see more conversions, Lord God. You alone know how often we have sinned in wandering from Your ways. We worship You, and humble ourselves before You. Thank You for hearing our prayer in Jesus' name. Amen.

God of grace help us to admit our sin, so that we may repent, turn to You, and receive forgiveness. Glory, honor, and praise belong to You. Thank You for redeeming us. Grant that members will be prepared for persecution, remembering to love, not curse, their persecutors, if and when the time comes. Be glorified in Jesus' name we pray. Amen.

226

Praise be to You forever, eternal God. We pray our church community will grow more distinct from the world in love and holiness, even as it engages our larger community. Thank You for being our strength and our shield. We have not done justice, loved kindness, or walked humbly with You, our God. We so much love being Your people, and we pray in Jesus' name. Amen.

227

We worship You in Your holy spirit and in the truth embodied in Jesus, our Lord. Have mercy on us, O merciful God, in Your loving-kindness. In Your great compassion, cleanse us from our sin. Thank You. We pray that the church's prayers would be infused with biblical ambitions, honesty, and humility. We offer this prayer in the power of Jesus' holy name. Amen.

228

Create in each of us a clean heart, Lord, and renew right spirits within each heart. Thank You for sending Jesus, O God, Who teaches us how to pray. Please grant that the church's songs would teach our members to biblically confess, lament, and praise as well as pray. Grant that each may learn a lifestyle of prayer, as we pray now in Jesus' name. Amen.

Is there anyone like You, Lord? You are a God of mighty acts. Empower the preaching of Your Word, that it is biblically careful and Holy Spirit imbued. Thank You for fulfilling Your promises in Jesus. We confess our sinfulness, our shortcomings, and our offenses against You. Glory, praise, and worship can only be about You. We offer this prayer in the power of Jesus' name. Amen.

230

We know You always listen to us, loving Father, and we want to listen to You. We are sinners, yes, but do not cast us away from Your presence, or take Your Holy Spirit from us. Thank You for being so forgiving and gracious. We pray that transparent, meaningful relationships would become normal and remaining anonymous becomes strange. We offer our prayer in Jesus' name. Amen.

231

Almighty and loving God, we love how You have given us eyes to see Your light to fill our lives. We pray our leaders will remain above reproach, and they be kept from temptation, complacency, idols, and worldliness. Blot out our sins, restore in us the joy of Your salvation, and sustain us with Your bountiful Spirit. We adore You, we thank You, and we pray in Jesus' name. Amen.

232

God of grace, You have made our minds, so we want to know You. We pray that a hunger for studying the gospel would form among us so that we can guide and guard one another in it. We are grateful for wanting that hunger. Forgive our sins and help us to live in Your light, and to walk in Your ways, for love's sake of Jesus Christ our Savior. Amen.

In Your love, heavenly Father, You have made our voices, so now we sing Your praise. For wasting Your gifts, and forgetting Your love, have mercy on us, for we are ashamed of all we have done to displease You. Thank You for the mercy of Jesus' blood. We pray faithful leaders will emerge to use Scripture to train members for the work of ministry. We offer our hearts in Jesus' name. Amen.

234

We surrender what we are and have to You in the name of Your Son, Jesus. Increase our faith, to strengthen us to better serve You. We need more chances when we fail You to fulfill Your purposes for us. We praise You and love You. You are gloriously at work among us, using us for Your awesome glory. For this & much more we are thankful, and we pray in Jesus' name. Amen.

235

We are amazed You love us despite our sins because Jesus died for our us. Your unrelenting love inspires us and humbles us, Heavenly Father. Thank You for being so patient and merciful towards us. For each of us in our spiritual community, we ask that You be our shield and fortress. For hearing our prayers for healing, mercy, and grace, in Jesus' name. Amen.

236

We're Yours through Jesus as our Lord and Savior, Lord God. We need Your mercy and grace, for we often sin against You, even unintentionally. Thank You for not giving up on us. Amid the messes we make, help us stay focused upon You. We humbly ask You to teach us how to serve You better on Your terms, Your way, in Jesus' name. Amen.

We humbly ask You to hear our prayer, Loving God. Please keep our eyes open to where You're leading us, since we don't know all that You know. We know we need Your forgiveness and grace. We're in awe of You, and praise and worship You. Thank You for delivering another tomorrow, another chance, we pray in the name of our risen Savior and Lord, Jesus Christ. Amen.

238

We are unworthy of Your reckless love, Gracious God. Your work among us is amazing, as You bind us together as a community of faith. We're thankful that You have never given up on us. Merciful God, use us to glorify Yourself, for sometimes we feel so immersed in this sin-filled world that we hunger for Your presence and truly long to see You glorified in Jesus' name. Amen.

239

Heavenly Father, we certainly don't deserve Your loving mercy and grace. We surrender the future to You. Please comfort those we know who are in pain and heal them. Thank You for another chance to walk with Jesus today and learn from Him. We surrender the challenges we are facing to You, Father. In the power of Jesus' name, we offer our prayer. Amen.

240

We gladly surrender it all we are to You, Lord God. Please help us to prepare fully for what lies ahead. We have not been keeping our eyes on You while helping others in Your name. Ever-loving God, Your patience and mercy are easily as amazing as Your grace. Thank You for bringing us to this day, delivering us from the evil in our world. We offer this prayer in Jesus' name. Amen.

Merciful God, we confess we could do more than we are doing. We love and adore You, eternal and humbling God. We're grateful for those saints now in heaven who have gone before us to create and build our spiritual community. Help our community of faith to be more like Our Savior and Lord. We humbly offer our prayers to Your perfect timing in Jesus' name. Amen.

242

We let go of our concerns for the future of our spiritual community to You, gracious God. We ask You to multiply our efforts to serve You and worship You. Thank You for being our good shepherd and watching over our family and friends who have gone astray. Our faith is sometimes weak, but You are our strength. In the name of Jesus, we love You and praise You. Amen.

243

Awesome God, You amazingly set and defend our boundaries as our shield and fortress. Forgive us when we forget we are forgiven. Thank You for sustaining us. We ask for Your healing and redemption for those we know to be sick or in pain, either physically or mentally. You, Lord, are greater than our fears as You continue to love us, so we surrender our fears to You in the power of Jesus' name. Amen.

244

We need Your forgiveness and grace, merciful heavenly Father. The wondrous beauty of Your creation, all around us, reminds us how much we need You. Thank You for being so patient and kind. Please guide and empower us to be Your church, sharing the gospel and Your holy love. All the praise and glory belong to You, and we pray in Jesus' name. Amen.

We give all that we are and have to You, gracious heavenly Father. We pray for our family and neighbors. Some of them can be difficult to love, so help us to love each of them as You teach us to do. You have shown us how to serve You on Your terms, in Your way. Thank You. Forgive our sometimes-clumsy efforts. We offer this prayer to Your power and love in Jesus' name. Amen.

246

Heavenly Father, we cannot even begin to love You as much as You love us or praise You enough. We're sorry when we are inconsistent in our praise. Thank You for the ability to perceive so much of You around us. Help us to see more clearly the path You have prepared for each of us. We humbly offer this prayer, knowing that You are and supply all that is good. Amen.

247

We don't express our love and appreciation for You enough, Father in heaven. Please multiply our efforts to do Your will, making, maturing, and multiplying faithful disciples in Your church. We ask for Your mercy, for we often stumble and fail to be faithful. Your love, Lord God, fuels our faith gives us passion to serve You. We offer this prayer seeking the power and glory of Jesus forever. Amen.

248

Your unrelenting love and grace are amazing, O God. Please strengthen our efforts to start new programs with Your nurture and guidance. Though we want more than we need, thank You for supplying our needs. We need Your forgiveness every day. We're devoted to You, and we adore You and our Lord Jesus. We pray in the power of His name. Amen.

We honor and adore You with our worship, Holy Father. We cling to Your mercy and grace, knowing that You sent Jesus to save us. Thank You for giving us more chances to do Your will, sharing both the gospel and Your holy love. We know some who need an extra measure of Your grace and ask for their healing. We humbly offer our prayer in Jesus' name. Amen.

250

Just as we are, we offer ourselves to You, Gracious God. Please help us make, mature, and multiply more faithful disciples of Jesus that are born again. We depend upon You to save us from our sins, Lord Jesus. You gloriously rule our community of faith with mercy and grace. Thank You for multiplying our efforts to serve You in Your name. Amen.

251

Our shortcomings plague us, Lord Jesus, and we cling to You to save us. We are in awe of You, for You are gloriously changing the world through Your church. Thank You for being our fortress, and deliverer. Please help us grow into becoming more like You as we follow You. May our gracious God be in control, guiding us. We ask our prayer in Jesus' name. Amen.

252

Gracious God, You hold our future through Jesus, our Savior. Help us strain out the truth from the waterfall of words coming from our media. Thank You for hearing all our prayers and answering out of Your kindness and mercy. Your Son shed his blood to wash away our many sins, saving us. Our Father, we are Yours, and we want to serve You Your way. We pray through Jesus, amen.

We joyfully take in the beauty of all of Your creation, gracious and eternal God. Forgive us, for we don't do the things we should do, and we do things we didn't intend to do. Thank You for being so patient with us. We ask for the vision to perceive Your will, and we're glad You're helping us grow in our faith. All praise and glory belong to You, through Jesus, our Savior. Amen.

254

We depend on You, Almighty God and we are standing on Your promises. We pray for our family and friends who haven't accepted Jesus as their Savior, that they may come to know Him. We still need Your forgiveness for our shortcomings. Thank You for not giving up on us and giving us more chances. We continue to pray in Jesus' name. Amen.

255

When our thoughts turn to evil and away from You, merciful Father in heaven, please forgive us. We love You, Almighty God and Father of our Savior, Jesus. Thank You for the many saints before us that originated our current community of faith. Please increase our faith and our trust in You, Gracious God. In Your divine care are All that we are and have. It is through Jesus our Lord we pray. Amen.

256

Our every thought is known to You, amazing and awesome God. From weeds to great trees Your glory shines through Your creation. We need Your mercy and grace every day because of our sins. Thank You for the everyday blessings we too easily take for granted. Grant us the wisdom to respond quickly to the many needs around us. Use us for Your glory, we ask in Jesus' name. Amen.

Heavenly Father, we praise You seven days, not just Sundays. Please show us how to live out Your plans and purposes for our lives. Our failures remind us that You redeem us through Jesus' blood, and our sins remind us of Your perfection. We offer ourselves to You in Jesus' name. Thank You for being our shield and fortress. Amen.

258

When we have turned a blind eye to sin, Father, please forgive us. We're thrilled with the new life that constantly grows around us. Thank You for hearing our prayers, even when we don't see the answers. Thank You for protecting the innocent we know. You alone are all that is good and right. We surrender them into Your hands in the name of Jesus, our Savior and Lord. Amen.

259

We bind our hearts to Your love, Gracious Father, for You bind us together with that eternal love. Be our shield and fortress and guide us to respond faithfully to Your leading. Thank You for Your loving presence. We're sorry we often don't notice the evidence of Your work in our midst. We offer our prayer in Jesus' name. Amen.

260

You, Father in heaven, are the creator and redeemer of everything. Please let each of us walk each day with Jesus as our constant companion. Please forgive us even when we're tempted to extreme responses to the evil that can be as bad as the evil itself. Thank You for being so patient with us. We offer this prayer in Jesus' holy name. Amen.

We are glad we're forgiven through Jesus' blood shed on the cross, for our shortcomings are manifested every day. We praise You and glorify You from our hearts. We're grateful that You have delivered us from so much evil and thankful we are so abundantly blessed. Please show us Your way into our future. We lay our burdens before You in Jesus' name. Amen.

262

We yield to Your divine authority, O wondrous God. We grieve with You over those who respond to violent injustice with more raging injustice. Put Your word on our lips to respond. Thank You for leading us through recent challenges. We certainly don't deserve all that You provide us out of Your abundant love. We look to our Jesus that we follow, and we pray this in our Savior's name. Amen.

263

We humbly kneel before You and worship, heavenly Father. We confess we're sometimes tempted to respond to evil with unrighteous anger. Please forgive us. Thank You for picking us up when our faith falters. Deliver us, Lord God, for the world around us seems out of control. Please lead us with Your everlasting light in the name of Your Son Jesus. Amen.

264

If You had not sent Jesus to die for us, Holy Father, we would be so utterly lost in this temptation-filled world. Our praise goes beyond Sunday mornings and into the entire week. Thank You for being ready to forgive us again whenever we ask. Please teach us to worry less and trust You more. We give over control into Your almighty hands in Jesus' name. Amen.

Gracious God, You are in charge, and we thank You for hearing our prayers. Please guide us past the maze of lies and other evils that assault our lives through the media. Thank You for Your compassion towards us. So often we sin against You, not just in what we do, but even in what we think and say. We offer ourselves to You again in Jesus' name. Amen.

266

Beloved Lord God, we're so often weak, but You are always strong. So often we fail to love You and each other in our church community unconditionally. Please mercifully forgive us. Thank You for teaching us Your better ways. Grow in us faith that is warm, strong, peaceful, and compassionate. We surrender to You, just as we are, in Jesus' name. Amen.

267

All praise and glory are Yours, heavenly Father. Increase our faith, Lord, and strengthen us to do Your will. We don't have Your patience, and sometimes we just don't want to forgive politicians and others who keep us from moving forward. Beautiful Creator and Savior, we find real joy in walking with Jesus, for we want to be completely His and faithfully witness through Him in His name. Amen.

268

We surrender our hurts, habits, and hang-ups to You, merciful God. Take away the ugliness in us as sinners and recreate within us a measure of Your beauty. We are grateful that You guide us through our world's chaos. You mercifully forgive us through Jesus' blood, even though we have no excuses for our sins, and we are amazed. All blessings flow from You, for we pray in Jesus' name. Amen.

We see the beauty of Your creation all around us, Lord God, when we pause to look beyond ourselves. We too often lose track of Your plans and purposes for us as Your church. Thank You for being our fortress and shield. Help us to make, mature, and multiply more faithful followers of our Lord Jesus more productively. We give You all that we are in Jesus' name. Amen.

270

Heavenly Father, we find joy in seeing You glorify Yourself in our spiritual community. Sometimes we act as though we don't know You and know Your ways. Please forgive us. We join countless others in Heaven and on Earth in praising You. Thank You for setting us free from our spiritual bondage to the things we love instead of loving You, and we offer our prayer in Jesus' name. Amen.

271

As sinners, merciful God, we are both encouraged and held accountable because we're forgiven by Your grace. We love You, gloriously awesome God. Thank You for having unique plans and purposes for each of us. Please provide healing and redemption to those we know who need You. We surrender all that we are, along with what we take for granted in Jesus' name. Amen.

272

Wondrous Father in heaven, we adore You for common things like a night full of stars and gentle wind in the trees. We don't deserve Your forgiveness and grace. It is a privilege to live as well as we do. Thank You for abundantly supplying our needs. Please help us to love the people we don't know yet who need Jesus. We offer our prayers and ourselves in Jesus' name. Amen.

Loving Father in heaven, our love for You seems so puny by comparison. We lift up to You those in the news who make us mad, sad, or both. Forgive us. They need Jesus as much as we do. Please grant us a measure of Your patience and teach us to be gracious. We love You Our Father, Our Savior, and the guidance and power of Your Spirit. We lift our prayers up in Jesus' name. Amen.

274

We adore being Yours, Lord Jesus, and we love learning to live as well as pray in Your name. Teach us to work together more effectively as a community of faith. Thank You, Heavenly Father, for healing beyond hurt, for Your love beyond measure, for life beyond life, and the mysteries beyond comprehending that You provide for us. Forgive us for taking these gifts for granted. Amen.

275

Thank You for clear night skies when we can witness the vastness of Your creation, mighty God. We complain too much about things we've given ourselves to do. Forgive us. Thank You for the breath we have to say thank You, and for friends who encourage us. Help us as a community of faith to encourage and support one another through each other's difficulties. We surrender our worries to Your almighty hands in Jesus' name. Amen.

276

Gracious God, all of Your creation is beautiful, from the sounds of singing birds to lakes and meadows dressed in fog. All of our hope is in You, Lord. Help us to hear the voices that remind us that we are accountable to You. We must confess and say we don't deserve Your blessings. We offer ourselves to You, just as we are through Jesus, our Savior. Amen.

We don't stop to appreciate Your glory enough, loving Father in heaven. Thank You for giving us the ability to smell our favorite foods and the privilege of praying through the night. Please let us take refuge in You when the media feed us painful messages. We lift up the sorrows and pains around us to You in Jesus' name. Amen.

278

We are filled with joy and praise for You, Lord Jesus. Help us to respond to the needs around us more lovingly and graciously. Thank You for opportunities to laugh and share food and fellowship. Forgive us when we seek guidance from friends and family before seeking You with prayer. We surrender our own needs to You through Jesus in His name. Amen.

279

Merciful God, praise and applause for You never seem quite enough, for our lives are energized by Your presence and power. We truly need Jesus' blood to wash away our sins. Thank You for the ears to hear Your message of hope, from Your holy Word, loud and clear. Magnificent and glorious God, we need to be together as a community to worship You, that we may support and encourage one another, and to hold each other accountable in Jesus' name. Amen.

280

Too easily, gracious God, we consume things in our world without pausing to appreciate that these blessings are from You. Father, we adore You and love seeing You glorified. Thank You for generously providing for us to run this race of life until it's won. Please help us face our new challenges with a measure of Your divine creativity. We humbly pray in Jesus name we pray. Amen.

In this community of faith, we are Yours, O God, and bound together with Your eternal love. Please empower our efforts. Thank You for the opportunities You give us to serve others in Your name. Your unworthy servants hunger for a sense of Your presence and power, and to forgive us yet again. We offer our hearts and prayers to You in Jesus' name. Amen.

282

You are all that is good, Lord God, and Your blessings often amaze us. We confess we're too often passive, and we fail to stand firm against evils. Forgive us. Thank You for providing us with voices to make joyful noises to praise You. Wondrously compassionate God, help us to be more courageous to confront wicked racism and gossip. We offer our prayer and ourselves to You in Jesus' name. Amen.

283

Loving Father, we praise You for creating us with the abilities to enjoy what we see, hear, taste, touch, and smell. Please help us to grow as we make, mature, and multiply more faithful followers of Jesus, Your only begotten Son. Please forgive our fumbling efforts. We love You, O God. Thank You for renewing our hope with another day of possibilities with the gifts You provide to us. We lift up our prayer in Jesus' name. Amen.

284

Almighty God, as Your unworthy servants, we praise and glorify You as we celebrate Jesus our Savior. Please keep showing us better ways to face the evils that assault us. Thank You for hearing our prayers, for the Deceiver can lead us astray without You. Despite our sins You keep surprising us with blessings. You deserve all the glory and praise as our victories are won through You. Amen.

Amazing Father, Your creation is glorious, with sunlight dancing through green trees waving at blue skies. Our common sin is we often assume the goodness You provide. Thank You! Help us to be more faithful as we draw our strength and health from Your true vine, our Savior Jesus. We are Yours through the power of Jesus' name. Amen.

286

Eternally present Father in heaven, we hunger for You, for You have given us this beautiful life. We lift up to You our country's overwhelming problems, for too easily we can become part of them. Please forgive us. Nothing is too difficult for You, and we depend upon You as we battle our world's evils. Thank You for working to finish what You've started in us. In Jesus' name we thank You. Amen.

287

We keep forgetting to thank You, gracious heavenly Father, for things we take for granted. We love the quiet times to be in His presence, being nourished by Your Holy Spirit. Thank You for the sunrise of another day. Please strengthen us to stand together as a community of faith. We love Your constantly helping us to stay focused upon Your ways and purposes. We offer ourselves and our prayers in Jesus' name. Amen.

288

Loving God, Your mercy and grace are amazing. You know us better than we know ourselves, yet You are merciful, gracious, and loving. Thank You for being our shield and fortress. We cling to You with our desire to offer kindness and love to those suffering around us. All glory, honor, and praise belong to You through our Lord Jesus, Amen.

Please show us ways You can use us to bring healing and peace to the community around us. We give our uncertainties and cares to You. Please forgive our often-clumsy efforts to serve You, loving Father, in the midst of our wonderful country that You nourish so beautifully. Thank You for hearing our prayers and responding in Your faultless way with Your perfect timing. Amen.

290

Holy God, in the wake of ongoing crisis, we're even more aware of our sinful thoughts that betray us. We offer all that we are to You, our merciful God. Thank You for being our deliverer and fortress against evil. As our world surrounds us with evil deceptions and uncertainty, please guide us and deliver us as we make our way into the future, in the name of Jesus, our Lord and Savior. Amen.

291

Heavenly Father, please continue to guide our community of faith and multiplying our efforts, to glorify You. Thank You for being so patient with us. Too often our shortcomings and weaknesses seem to hold us back from serving You as we want to do. Use us for Your glory and help us to move in mission more effectively to our community, we ask in Jesus' name. Amen.

292

Gracious God, all that we are and have are Yours. Your mercy and grace are amazing. Please show us ways You can use us to bring healing and peace to our community. We're aware of our sinful thoughts that betray us. All glory, honor, and praise belong to You through our Lord Jesus. Thank You for being so patient with us. We offer our prayer in Jesus' name. Amen.

Your mercy surpasses all of our sins, heavenly Father. Thank You, Lord, for You are the source of all of our blessings, none of which we deserve. Thank You for redeeming us from so much wickedness. Keep reminding us that we have an unseen enemy who wants to separate us from You. We give our uncertainties and cares to You, in the name of Jesus, our Lord and Savior. Amen.

294

We often worry about our health and that of those we love, so we submit them to Your healing and redemption. We surrender to Your protection and loving care. Thank You for providing for us to be forgiven through Jesus' death on the cross. Thank You for hearing our prayers and responding in Your faultless way with Your perfect timing, Lord Jesus, in Your name. Amen.

295

All-knowing glorious God, there's no corner so dark You do not see, no whisper so soft You cannot hear. We sin against You unintentionally and need the power of Jesus' shed blood to save us. Thank You for saving us from ourselves and forgive us, Lord. Our country is undeniably polarized. We ask for Your wisdom to determine what is true and right. It is in the name of Jesus, Your Son, and our Savior that we pray. Amen.

296

We're sorry we don't spend more time seeking You, loving Father, but instead we wait until it is convenient. To You, Jesus, belongs all praise, glory, and honor. Thank You for guiding and empowering us as we follow Jesus. We ask You to help us start fresh as we move ahead because Your Word says You make all things new. We're humbled by the power in Jesus' name as we pray. Amen.

Glorious Father in heaven, please let there be peace again in our country, and let it begin with us. Use us, we pray, for Your glory through Jesus. Thank You for more chances to be like Him. Forgive us. Our secret sins can't be hidden from You. Please help us to learn from these recent days, and to prepare wisely for what lies ahead. Our future is in Your almighty hands. Amen.

298

Amazingly gracious God, we praise You for binding us to Yourself and to each other with Your love. We're sinners who need Your salvation in Jesus' blood that was shed for us. Thank You for letting Jesus' love flow so freely among us. Please increase our sometimes faltering and weak faith, for we depend upon You. We pray in Jesus' mighty name. Amen.

299

Almighty and eternal God, help us to be kind like Jesus in the midst of difficult people. They challenge us to live out our faith and share the gospel with them. Please forgive our often-clumsy efforts to serve You. When we thirst for You, we find Your Living Water, Jesus, and we praise You for His presence. Thank You for delivering us and forgiving us, we pray in our Savior's name. Amen.

300

Please help us let go of what has passed, O God, and move into the future with our Savior. We offer all we are. Thank You for Your new mercies and grace – sometimes we get discouraged. Forgive us for taking Your peace for granted when life seems easy. Gracious God, we praise You for providing our Prince of Peace, who is so welcome to live within us. It is in Jesus' name we pray. Amen.

Wondrous God, we worship and love You. Forgive us, out of Your divine mercy, when we idolize people we know or the things we have. Thank You for providing for all of our real needs. Please teach us to pray with less doubt, help our unbelief, and have greater faith in You. We offer our prayers that You may be glorified through the power of Jesus' name. Amen.

302

Loving heavenly Father, please continue to show us Your ways in Jesus' life. We offer ourselves and our spiritual community to You. Forgive us for focusing on our feet instead of looking ahead and to You. We praise You, Father, for new life and fresh opportunities. Thank You for leading us and protecting us during difficult days. We offer our prayer in Jesus' name. Amen.

303

We're sinners, heavenly Father, and it makes it easier to forgive each other knowing You have forgiven us through Jesus' death on the cross. We offer our hearts to You, for it is His sacrifice that makes us one as a church. Thank You for hearing us. Grant that we may clearly see the path You've prepared for us, for Your way is always better. Without You, we are nothing, but with You, everything is possible through Jesus' name. Amen.

304

We praise You, Lord God almighty, for Your unrelenting and forgiving love. Please forgive us for not trusting in You more. Thank You for using us for Your glory as we live out the gifts You've given us. Please let us lean on You as we take uncertain steps into our future, hoping that we're not making mistakes. We surrender the challenges we face with prayer in Jesus' name. Amen.

We offer our hearts to You, O Lord, for You alone are our fortress, delivering us from evil. Help us to be the church You want us to be. Forgive us, Father, when we don't step out in faith with You. We find our rest, joy, and all that is good in You. Thank You for experiences that lead us to trust You more, and for teaching us to serve You on Your terms. We serve and pray in Jesus' name Amen.

306

Eternal God our Father, we know You hear our prayers, but often we pray with doubt. Forgive us. We praise You, loving God, for the glories of Your creation. We certainly don't deserve the blessings that are ours and don't earn. Thank You for Your patience with us. May Your praise always be on our lips, Father, in the name of Jesus and in the power of Your Holy Spirit we pray. Amen.

307

Father in heaven, our fears and worries we put into Your hands, in the name of Your son, Jesus. Help us to be more faith-filled with our Savior, for we are His. We're thankful that we can depend upon Your faithfulness. Heavenly Father, we confess we're often impatient with Your perfect timing. We surrender to You and Your ways, Father, in the power of Your son's name, Jesus, Amen.

308

We know we're not worthy to serve You, merciful God in heaven, yet You love us and call us to serve You anyway. We praise You for all that You are – Creator, Son, and Holy Spirit. Thank You for making things new and fresh. Keep prompting us to share the good news with those who are lost. We surrender our worries and fears to You in Jesus' name. Amen.

We bask in Your glory and Your gracious love, heavenly Father. Forgive us, merciful God, for we don't seek Your presence and power more throughout each day. Thank You for delivering us from evil threats, both visible and invisible. You have called us to serve You, and we gladly obey, empowered by the power of Jesus' name. Amen.

310

Father, You amaze us with the glories of Your creation, while we're standing in man-made messes. Please keep our eyes and ears clear to stay on the path You've prepared for us. We're sorry, God of mercy, that often we don't see Your gifts in the middle of our pains and struggles. We praise and adore You, Father. Thank You for providing us with our example to follow. In His name we pray. Amen.

311

Heavenly Father, when our prayers are answered, it makes You seem more glorious. Please keep reminding us that You're with us in our storms and battles. Thank You for helping us keep our heads held high as we walk through the storms of our lives. We need Jesus' blood to cleanse us of our sins as much as ever. Before we were conceived, Father, You had plans and a purpose for each of us, so we follow Jesus, and in His name we pray. Amen.

312

Heavenly Father, we praise You with new songs in our mouths. Forgive us when we doubt Your faithfulness even while we are faithless. Thank You for our countless second chances to serve You more faithfully. Please help us make, mature, and multiply more faithful followers of Jesus, for by His authority, we grow His church and in His name we pray. Amen.

We give praise and glory to You, Holy Spirit, as You guide and empower us. Please teach us, Gracious God, to bring healing and redemption to those in need. We give You all that we are in response to Your calls upon us, giving us life in Jesus. As we move ahead, we know we cannot return to the past, so help us find new ways to serve You and give You glory in Jesus' name. Amen.

314

You, merciful God, are our fortress amidst the storms of life. As we move forward into the future You have prepared for us, please help us stay focused upon You. Thank You for not giving up on us and being patient. To our shame, we never quite trust You enough. Forgive us. Our lives are on our Lord Jesus, Your son, and in His name we pray. Amen.

315

Forgive us, Lord Jesus, when we focus on our struggles and not on our blessings. Yesterday's worries no longer matter, and tomorrow is in Your hands. Whether in the heat of summer or the frost of winter, Lord, thank You for providing glorious and amazing life for us. Please help us to continue growing in our faith in You. We can face anything today, Lord Jesus, because You are our strength, and our prayers are in Your name. Amen.

316

Glorious and humbling God, we offer our hearts to You because You give us so much. Help us, Lord, to be more effective and productive at making faithful disciples of our Savior, Jesus. Thank You for past saints who have prepared our way. Our present shortcomings betray us. Forgive us. Your ways are better than ours, and we pray in Your name. Amen.

We're sorry we complain so easily, merciful God, while Your blessings are abundant. Forgive us. Our hearts filled with praise come from our love for You, Lord. Thank You for the opportunities You're giving us for making new friends who we can lead to Jesus. Help us to make the most of what we have as we show others Your salvation, love, and grace. In Jesus' name we praise You, Amen.

318

Yours is the power, glory, and majesty in Your Holy Trinity, O God. We know that Your blood that was shed for us cleanses us from our daily sins. Thank You for leading us into a life worth living and having a purpose. Our hearts are Yours because You have provided our salvation through Jesus. We live and pray in the power of His name. Amen.

319

We ask that You show us the best ways reach souls who are lost and help grow those who are learning to follow You. We offer our hearts to You, Lord, that we may be faithful. You continue to be merciful despite our sins and shortcomings. Thank You for supplying us with more possibilities for renewed life when we think we're almost out. We love You and praise You in the name of Jesus, Our Savior. Amen.

320

Glory and praise come from our voices naturally, Lord God. We're sorry we've ignored chances to share Your holy love and salvation. Thank You for saving us from trying to restore past plans and habits in our past. Show us Your ways into our future as a community of faith. We offer what we are and have to You in the name of Your son Jesus, our Savior. Amen.

Gracious heavenly Father, we can praise You regardless of what happens. Show us, Lord, more effective ways to fulfill Your mission You have in us, for our community. Thank You for loving us despite ourselves. We put on a good front before friends and family, but we can't hide any shameful thing from You. Forgive us. We offer our prayers in the name of Jesus. Amen.

322

We don't deserve Your blessings, merciful God, as we continue to be sinners needing Your forgiveness. We love You, Father, and we honor and praise You through Your Son, Jesus. We thank You for Your patience with us, as we often fumble opportunities You supply us. Please increase our faith, that we may serve You more effectively. We humbly offer our prayer in Jesus' name. Amen.

323

Despite challenges, we catch glimpses of Your glory, Lord, so we love and bless You, O God. Grant us the wisdom to discern facts amidst opinions as we face each of evil's challenges. We're sinners, but Your gracious love flows steadily and dependably, as You forgive and redeem us. The Youngest apostle of Jesus says You are love, and we love You. We thank You with our prayer in Jesus' name. Amen.

324

Father in heaven, we're sorry we often miss seeing what You are doing. It is excellent when we're still and know Your presence, Lord God. Thank You for nudging us onto our current path as a community of faith. Grant us a measure of Your wisdom to discern how we must respond to our community's needs. Use us for Your glory as we follow the lead of Your Son, in whose name we pray. Amen.

Alleluia! We truly belong to You, our Creator, Your son, Jesus, and Your Holy Spirit, and we're Your family. Through Jesus' blood we're forgiven of our sins, so we cannot thank You enough. Help us to be kind and loving towards those outside our church, including those hard to love, and help us lead them to Jesus, in His name we pray. Amen.

326

We're Yours as a community of faith, O heavenly Father. Help us to better serve You when things seem chaotic, for we hunger to see You glorified. Forgive us when we get overwhelmed instead of asking for Your divine help. We've learned it is worth the effort to seek You first. Saying thank You hardly seems enough, so we simply offer our prayer in Jesus' name. Amen.

327

We love giving our loyalty to You, our loving heavenly Father, because of Your divine faithfulness. Guide our feet to keep following You, we pray. Thank You for giving our faith community the vision to perceive Your will and the ever-increasing faith to trust in You. Sometimes our pasts seem to haunt us, so we need Your grace as well as Your forgiveness. We adore placing our trust in You and Your divine timing through Jesus. Amen.

328

We love You, heavenly Father, and You have our hearts and hands to serve You. Bring us together with others that need to know Our Savior, Jesus. Thank You for the vision to see where You're leading us. The Enemy of our souls still tries to deceive us. Forgive us when we take our eyes off You. We offer ourselves to You through the power of Jesus' name. Amen.

Forgive us, loving Father, we sometimes worry when a dream You've given us isn't fulfilled quickly. We know we can always trust You. Glorious God, it is Your eternal love that binds us to You and to each other. Thank You for being forgiving and patient towards us. Help us to unite our individual gifts to serve You as one. We offer ourselves with our prayers in Jesus' name. Amen.

330

True freedom is ours as we walk by faith in You, glorious God. Our coins say we trust You, but forgive us, for we often don't show it. Thank You for providing for us even as You deliver us from evils around us. Help us to pick up the pieces of our broken dreams, and show us Your better way. We offer ourselves again in service to You in His name. Amen.

331

We adore You passionately, Father God, and we pause simply to be present to Your presence and power. Help us remember that service is about serving You, and it is not about us. Forgive us, Heavenly Father, when we fail to focus on the plans and purposes You have for us separately as well as together. We belong to Jesus and pray in His name. Amen.

332

All we are, we offer to You, heavenly Father. When soldiers feel weary, we ask that You refresh their strength. We all thoughtlessly pursue perfection in ourselves when You simply ask us to pursue Jesus' holiness. Your caring patience with us moves us to love You more and more, Lord. Thank You for delivering us from evils that so often plague where we live. We ask this in Jesus' name. Amen.

We praise You with music and worship, glorious God, and we love You. Bless and protect those in our military Lord and use their work for the good of our nation and Your glory. Thank You, Lord, for using the bravery of men and women as part of Your protection for us. We're tempted to worry about what this day may hold. You're our shield and fortress. We're Yours in Jesus' name. Amen.

334

Help us forgive ourselves for past mistakes, gracious God. It is wonderful to be loved by You, Lord. Thank You for giving us more second chances. For those who serve our country in the military, we pray that they would be filled with Your strength flowing through them. We offer all that we are with our prayer support for them in the power of Jesus' name. Amen.

335

Heavenly Father, we know we're sinners who need Your forgiveness. Thank You for patiently turning our gaze back upon Jesus. We pray for the protection of our armed forces as they serve our country around the world right now. We thank You for the military's sacrificial service on our behalf. We offer ourselves and our prayers to You, Father, in the power of Jesus' name. Amen.

336

Lord God, we offer our hearts to You. Hear our prayer of thanks for our veterans who made great sacrifices on our behalf. We ask that You bless them and meet all their needs. Thank You for opportunities to escape all distractions and enjoy Your holy presence. We foolishly think we're alone in our battles against evil. Forgive us. We love You and pray in Jesus' name. Amen.

Forgive, redeem, and restore us when we have sinned against You, merciful Father. We love You, even as You use us for Your glory. Thank You. When sailors feel isolated, we ask that You give them the assurance that You are with them. You have so amazingly equipped all of us to serve You Your way. We offer ourselves with this prayer in Jesus' name. Amen.

338

Be glorified, heavenly Father, as we offer You our best efforts, accepting new challenges. Forgive us when we shift our focus from You to ourselves and our own needs. Thank You for using us as a community of faith to share the gospel with others as we encourage one another. Multiply our efforts to serve You as we share the good news of Jesus, our Savior, in whose name we pray. Amen.

339

We are Yours, Lord Jesus, and we love You. We ask You to work through and in us as You set people free from their bondage to the Father of Lies, who has sometimes deceived us. Empower and guide us to fulfill the dreams You've given us and sow the seeds of Your gospel. We thank You and glorify You, and the Father, and the Holy Spirit as we pray. Amen.

340

Almighty God, may the airmen's and airwomen's work and mission for our country be successful. We love it when You use our military men and women for Your good purposes. Thank You for shedding Your light into the darkness to reveal the path You've prepared. Help us to focus clearly on the plans You have for us and to fulfill Your purposes. We offer our prayer in Jesus' name. Amen.

Loving God, we genuinely appreciate Your using us for Your purposes to help people in our community. Forgive us when we're enslaved to our past instead of seeking our future in You. Thank You for showing us new ways to be Your church. Help us to do our part to fulfill Your plans for our community of faith. You are already at work in our lives. We pray in Jesus' name. Amen.

342

We offer to serve You Your way, Heavenly Father. Grant us the vision to perceive Your will, and then increase our faith to believe in the vision You've given us. Forgive us the times we prayed as though giving You orders, Lord. We sing Your praises and declare our love for You. Thank You for showing us how to love people just as they are the way Jesus did. We pray in His name. Amen.

343

Knowing our weaknesses, Lord Jesus, we give ourselves to You. Help us, to face our hidden prejudices and find unity in Your cross as our equalizer. Thank You for being ready to listen to our prayers. We fail You often, while You are patient and kind, and Your love never fails. We're in awe of You and of Your love, and we love being present to Your presence. We pray in Your name. Amen.

344

We're sorry we confuse dreams for ourselves with Your plans for us, heavenly Father. We worship You and bless You. We thank You, and we love Jesus because He first loved us through His life, death, and resurrection. Please continue to be patient and kind towards us, even when we go astray from what Jesus teaches us. We offer our prayers in Your Son's name. Amen.

We offer You what we have and are, heavenly Father. As we study Your Word and worship, please open our eyes to see Your light in our darkness. We confess our doubts sometimes hold us back from seeing Your glory. Our hearts are Yours because all things are possible with You. Thank You for generously and tolerantly guiding us towards the holiness of Jesus, for it is in His name we pray. Amen.

346

We surrender to Your mercy and grace, Almighty God. Since You hold the future, we ask that You guide our often-uncertain steps amidst the many voices telling us what we can and cannot do. Thank You for fresh life each morning. We know our sin and try to please You, but we still stumble. We adore our Savior and King, who guides us into eternity, for it is in Jesus' name we pray. Amen.

347

You have many reasons to judge us, so we praise You for sending Jesus to pay debts to You. That glory and praise belong to our Savior. Thank You for lovingly sending Jesus to live, die, and rise from the dead for us. Bless our governments' leaders to do what is right and not just what's expedient. We offer this prayer in the power of Jesus' name. Amen.

348

We love You and worship You, glorious God, in the name of Your only begotten son, Jesus. Our sins and shortcomings still stain our lives with evil, so we need Jesus. Thank You for determining our path as a church and being our shield and fortress. Please challenge us with new ways to be Your church that witnesses and serves. You are gloriously wise and eternal, O God, and we offer our prayer in Christ's Holy name. Amen.

We offer ourselves to You, Lord God above, that You may use us for Your glory. We ask for opportunities today to lead people to Our Savior as we contribute to our spiritual community and beyond. Thank You for giving us more chances to serve You and thrive. We confess we tend to worry as we face our current challenges rather than as tests of our faith. In Jesus' name we pray. Amen.

350

Forgive our fear, O God, for we praise and adore You, as our Father, Savior, and Holy Spirit. We love the abundant life You have provided. Thank You. Increase our faith, that we may serve You more effectively, and make, mature, and multiply more faithful disciples of Jesus. We offer our prayers, Lord Jesus, because they are essential to our partnership with You. Amen.

351

Heavenly Father, knowing You through Jesus fills us with awe. Please forgive our empty glory when we idolize ourselves, our possessions, and our accomplishments. Thank You for calling us into Your family. Please let Jesus dwelling in our hearts empower us with strength and wisdom as we walk with Him into the future. We love You and need to trust You more as we pray in the power of Jesus' name. Amen.

352

We offer our love to You, our Heavenly Father, Your Jesus, and the Holy Spirit. We ask that You be with us as we face today's evils, just as You were with Your people as they entered the promised land. Thank You for Your faithfulness. We confess we've greedily asked for things we don't need. We love Your always standing by us as a faith community as we pray through Jesus' name. Amen.

We trust in You and love You, Heavenly Father. We're still sinners who need Christ's blood to cleanse us and redeem us. Thank You for sending Jesus to give us Your way, truth, and life. Please continue to put Your Holy Word on our lips and tasks to do Your way. We dedicate our time, talent, training, and resources to You, Father, and we pray in the name of Jesus. Amen.

354

Eternal God, We praise You and glorify You for looking beyond our sins because of Your love. Help us to look beyond the sources of lies to see Your truth, Your ways, and Your abundant life. Forgive our sometimes-shaky faith. Thank You for being our shield and being incredibly good and gracious towards us. In our Savior's name we pray. Amen.

355

Ever-faithful God, We regret our worries in light of Your faithfulness. Because of Your divine love, we are one in Your Spirit and one in Your love. Thank You for greater faith growing out of our previous doubts. Help us to teach others to seek You as we share the gospel in a language they can understand and embrace. We offer You our hearts through Jesus our Savior, and we pray in His name. Amen.

356

Almighty God, strengthen us emotionally and spiritually as walk with our Master and Savior. We consecrate ourselves to Jesus. Show us how to function as a family united in Your love. Thank You for being our warrior companion. We know we're still sinners, yet we're forgiven due to Jesus shedding His blood for us. You, Father, are glorious and amazing. In Jesus we pray. Amen.

We're Yours, loving heavenly Father. Help us understand how You want us to face our challenges and respond in faith. We confess our focus upon hoping You'll give us what we want rather than vice versa. Then we remember how graciously You supply our needs. We're thankful for having a new beginning, and a new path. We lift up our prayer in Jesus' name. Amen.

358

Forgive us, merciful heavenly Father, for we tend to cling to the past instead of trusting You with our future. We praise and love You as You bless us. Thank You for keeping us on the path You divinely prepared for us. Show us how we can better share the gospel and generously share the abundance You have given us. We offer ourselves just as we are, and we pray in Jesus' name. Amen.

359

We love experiencing Your divine presence, Gracious God, as we worship You and pray. Forgive us when we are worried, and don't trust in You. Thank You for being so patient and loving towards us despite our shortcomings. Show us Your way to adjust to the changes in our culture. We surrender to You the earthly things we hold dear in the name of Jesus. Amen.

360

Eternal God, our glorious Father, we love serving You and worshiping You. Be patient and forgive us, Lord, when we're scared of trying new things. Thank You for reassuring us in the Bible that all things are possible with You. Grant us the eyes to recognize Your will and the heart to comprehend Your still small voice as You lead us. We submit ourselves to serve You, O Lord of our hopes and future. Amen.

We surrender to Your perfect timing, eternal God. We love You and love all that You have done, filling us with joy, peace, patience, kindness, goodness, faithfulness, gentleness, and self-control. Thank You for supplying all of our needs. Help us show others that now is the perfect time to start following Jesus that they may join us joyfully. We offer You our hearts in the power of Jesus' name. Amen.

362

Gracious God of limitless possibilities, we offer our strength and time. Increase our faith, O God, for we know that what we gain in following and serving Jesus will endure forever. Thank You for drawing us into the cause of Christ. Forgive our sometimes-sour attitudes, even though we know we're Yours. We glorify Your name as we give You our best and pray in Jesus' name. Amen.

363

We adore You, mighty God, for You are our fortress, and we love Your standing with us as we face our challenges. Forgive our hesitation when our path seems dark. Thank You for the leadership we have from Jesus. Please equip us to accomplish what You are calling us to do, which is far more than we imagined. We're letting go of our pride and simply praying in Jesus' name. Amen.

364

We are embracing the new pathway You are revealing to us, glorious Father in heaven. Increase our courage and strengthen our faith in You. We love You and want the courage to trust You, but our faith is often weak. Forgive us. We remember how Your Son Jesus ordered the stormy sea to calm down with Your loving power. Thank You again for our salvation in Him. Amen.

Compared to the suffering we can see, gracious God in heaven, we live a life of blessing. Please help us finish what You've started in us and don't give up on us. Thank You for delivering us from evil and equipping us generously to sow the seeds of the gospel and serve our community. We know we're sinners, but we're cleansed by His blood. We humbly offer our prayer in Jesus' name. Amen.

366

In quiet with no distractions, we love enjoying Your presence and power, heavenly Father. Forgive us when we begin making demands before humbling ourselves before You. Thank You for being our Rock on which You have built Your church. Please draw us closer to Yourself as we read Your Word and pray. We surrender our clumsy efforts to Your guidance through Jesus, in whose name we pray. Amen.

Other Books by James J. Stewart
Available on Amazon
Christian Inspiration, Study, and Poetry

Faith and Yosemite:
Fourth Edition
[Christian poetry with pictures of Yosemite]
Faith Fuel
[Meditations on the Christian faith and life]
Lasting Love
[Short Biographical Sketches]
Living for Jesus
[A Gospels Study Guide for Couples and Small Groups]
Deliberately Growing Spiritually
[A five-year Bible reading program for spiritual transformation.]

Seed Thoughts for
Christian Prayer
and Meditation
[Workbook]
Single Sentence Sermons
[Workbook for growing faith]
Walking in Faith
[Much of the same poetry as Faith and Yosemite but without pictures]
Spiritually Growing Through Prayer
The focus is upon personal piety and spiritual growth through prayer.
In Jesus' Name
[Praying Effectively]

Christian Fiction

A Man, A Woman and a Cat
[A cheetah/Puma crossbreed brings together an architect and a famous actress.]
A Marriage of Miracles
[God sets up a whirlwind romance & fills two people's lives with miracles]
The Camera Doctors
[Two people meet on top a famous mountain, and romance ensues.]
Casting Lots
[Christian romance and adventure set in the near future]

Christian Romances in the Foothills
An anthology of Tom's Town, Soul Mates, & The Camera Doctors
An Extensive Life
[The life story of a man who lived more than four hundred years.]
Empty Tomb, Full Hearts
[A Selection of Testimonies Among Those Who Saw the Risen Christ]
The First Lady
[A brilliant musician and a brilliant astrophysicist stumble into politics, and they write new chapters of history.

The Gaardian Saga
[Christian science fiction fantasy involving God in a major role.]

God, Love, and Stargazing
God prepares two people for both romance and divine service.

A Nation Transformed
[A future tale of God intervening in the USA with miracles.

A Second Call to Serve
[A tenth-generation pastor and his second wife accept a call to build a church from scratch.]

Prayer Warriors
[Urban adventures in a near-future continuation of Casting Lots]

Soul Mates
[Romance, the same setting as Tom's Town]

This World Is Not My Home
[Two together since high school separate to find love with others.]

Tom's Town
[Small town life and Christian romance]

<u>*The Warrior and the Prophet*</u>
<u>*[God has surprises and blessings for newlyweds]*</u>

<u>Yosemite Picture Books</u>

Ever-Changing Yosemite Valley
[Yosemite Valley is a glacially carved valley. Moment by moment, scenes change.]

Faith and Yosemite Fourth Edition
[Pictures of Yosemite National Park, with poems about the Christian faith]

Portraits of El Capitan
[El Capitan rises 3000 feet above the floor of Yosemite Valley]

<u>*Portraits of Half Dome*</u>
[Half Dome marks the east end of Yosemite Valley]

A Sense of Wonder: Yosemite
[A Christian poem about Yosemite, illustrated with pictures]

Starlight Over Yosemite
[Large pictures of Yosemite taken at night]

Yosemite Textures and Shadows
[High definition photographs of Yosemite Valley, depicting all seasons, both day and night.]

www.ingramcontent.com/pod-product-compliance
Lightning Source LLC
Chambersburg PA
CBHW070855050426
42453CB00012B/2219